Wildest Dreams - Get Out of Your Own Way
Sarah Duff
Email: hello@yoursarahduff.com
Website: www.yoursarahduff.com
ISBN: 978-1-914933-39-4

Copyright 2022
All rights reserved. No part of this publication may be reproduced, stored in a retrieval system or transmitted in any form or by any means, electronic, mechanical, photocopy, recording or otherwise, without prior written consent of the copyright owner. Nor can it be circulated in any form of binding or cover other than that in which it is published and without similar condition including this condition being imposed on a subsequent purchaser.

The right of Sarah Duff to be identified as the author of this work has been asserted in accordance with the Copyright Designs and Patents Act 1988.

A copy of this book is deposited with the British Library

Published By: -

i2i
PUBLISHING

i2i Publishing. Manchester.
www.i2ipublishing.co.uk

Contents

Foreword	5
Introduction	17
Truth	41
Darkness	61
Light	99
Twin Flames	109
Karma	145
Magic	151
Embodiment	163
Wildest Dreams	185

Acknowledgement

The front cover design artwork is credited to the lovely Magdalena Nel Bliss, at https://nayamoonart.com
Thank you for giving me the permission to kindly share your divine, inspirational creativity.

Dedication

Dedicated to my children. Whom, one day, might want some help navigating any of their own missing jigsaw pieces, to help them unravel their own place and time in the universe.
I love you to the moon and back to infinity and beyond forever and ever.

Foreword

Feminine souls shake our world into balance,
Earth is home and so is infinity,
Evolution moves through you,
You are not alone,
A woman dedicated to truth and awakening,
Rooted in compassion,
Loyal to the source within us all,
Tired of limiting beliefs, contractions, and patterning?
Of that old chestnut- 'I'm not good enough!'
Longing for full embodiment of spirit as well as for all beings?
Practice the feminine way,
An all-inclusive in the body spirituality,
Beyond dogma,
Awakening a living breathing path created through you, as you,
You don't have to do it alone.
Express her,
Butterfly Woman,
Fly.

Let's think positive. Let go and
let God.

Dear friend,

This book is committed to you and your truth. May you be blessed to find some comfort within these pages and that my insights, from deep within my own inner landscape, touch you in some meaningful way. Like me, do you find it hard to choose the right words to say to someone at times, or give yourself permission to communicate what you really want to say, and often feel the sentiments way more? Most regularly, expressing yourself with a frustrated charge.

Writing helps me to express my thoughts and feelings and provides me with a safe space to honour who I am. I can express myself much clearer through my prose. Do you feel the same way?

Much love to you on your own special journey, with the unfolding of your own perfect story.

Behind every strong woman, there is a story that gave her no other choice.
Anon.

The Buddha once mentioned that 'Life is suffering,' because Buddhists believe in the cycle of samsara, which is the cycle of birth, life, death, and rebirth. This means that people will experience suffering many times over. All the things a person goes through in life causes suffering, and we cannot do anything about it.

To date, I have come to know that from my own experiences, of my infinite half a century around the sun, that life certainly does throws us some really challenging curve, stink bombs, that blow your reality up into smitheries! You know the sticky sort? That destroying death of a loved one, disease, sickness, divorce, a stressful house move, our children's break ups and downs, empty nest syndrome, suicide, alcohol or drug abuse, mental health issues, loss of your child or, redundancy, and most presently, the trials and tribulations of the you know what virus.

What I have come to understand is that there is so much intelligence to be found in the dark wisdom. So many 'spiritual' people look up to the light, wanting only the love and light, peace, positivity, happiness, and unity. Of course, I want this most of the time too. However, a fully whole and balanced individual will come to recognise the innate wisdom is derived and gained from the things the scare and challenge us the most. Anything painful that we experience, undoubtedly brings us into harmony. This might sound odd or even completely cuckoo. But for me, without these experiences we fully never know what it is like to live fully human and content to express (not supress, oppress, or repress) all facets of our psyche, nature, or messy, imperfectly perfect humanness. It teaches us to flex our resilient muscle to its maximum potential, that's what life's harsh lessons do. It's your choice how to respond or react. It's your choice to open your crystal heart mind to 'see' the wisdom and magic that lies there, which is often a dormant intuitive aptitude, long forgotten in most people who are plugged into the matrix. On the contrary, resting within that labyrinth, that spiralling network of unresolved mind, speak in a contracted inflexible body.

'Anyone can practice yoga, mind is not stiff, body is.'

Understanding this, is living rich.
      Likewise, when we can bow down to another, in compassion, understanding and offer our sincere empathy. Right there and then in that moment, we have healed a part of us through our ability to witness and offer our heart energy with an open, non-judgemental, supportive container of love. Listening and feeling are an art. Some experts call this being in a self-actualised state of being. But for me, it is simply adopting the language of love; that which is our highest currency to feel and heal. Lest we forget, during these challenging times when a psychological division has been persecuted throughout the world. Forcing many people into fight, fright, flee, fold, or

freeze syndrome. And yes, I do perceive that it is a syndrome which has been created to divide, control, and keep sedated humans confined to the foreboding cages of the mind. This has gone on for centuries under the guise of many carefully orchestrated forms; HIV, Gays, women who choose to terminate a pregnancy, racists and so many more 'groups' which have been targeted throughout the ages to attack one another. It is a deceitful, manipulating game.

Why? Ask yourself this question then take a moment to think about what would happen if everyone tuned to their greatest gift, their capacity to love one another. Can you imagine the power of that and what kind of a world would be created? Think Jennifer Rush, Power of Love!

I dearly loved and valued John Lennon's musical ideologies on life. It was such a shame that he was shot dead so violently and suddenly. His legacy has left us with some beautiful, thoughtful, and heart-warming words of wisdom. If only we didn't just sing these words about love and peace but instead, everyone took more positive action in a loving and kind way. Maybe then we wouldn't have food shortages and dire poverty and famine for so many. It seems while the rich are getting richer, the poor and getting poorer. Do you ever wonder like me, just what do the elite do all day long with all that money?

Anyway, going off on a teacher tangent, once again, no apologies here. But just as I wrote my first book, 'Beyond Gratitude' (some of you will have absorbed its musings by now) this book is writing me. Incidentally, did you spot the crafty twist in the storyline? Hideously sneaky.

Oddly or not, during the last 3 months of the heavily sedating 'lockdown' and after the dark, long nights and gloomy weather, I really didn't feel the capacity to write at all. I felt like sludge, totally uninspired and comatose like. Sleeping like a hibernating bear until mid-morning. Unable to do anything, and I did not and could not fight it. For I intuitively felt it was the collective consciousness at play, as if something far greater and completely out of my control was at drama here. Then, suddenly, almost magically, I stated getting up excitedly at 5am with a plethora of non-stop insights into what needed to be shared. Was I coming out of an unfathomable hibernation? Have you ever got the urge to do something, and you can't explain why? My energy seems to reflect the moon, amplifying every single emotion that wants to get flushed out when full and juicy? Waxing or waning. Or am I totally bonkers?

Spring has sprung and so with it, the I, the Sarah human form, like the new-born skipping lambs, bouncing gleefully along the fells. What a joy to feel more energised, and to open one's eyes in the morning feeling alive, awakening to each beautiful new day noticing shiny, bright buds, dewy meadows, and clear blue skies. Ahhh, bliss. Heaven really is a place on earth as Belinda Carlisle fabulously sings.

During these dark few months, God love my boyfriend for putting up with my randomness and keeping up with my many parts, and my complete self-absorption. Yet, I do the same for him too. Aren't we all many parts? At any given moment?

Often, when I go to bed at night and settle down, reflecting on my 'Daily Wins,' I notice the range of personas I've displayed throughout my day, then giggle to myself at the amount of expended energy used in keeping up with all those amazing human capabilities. It's funny to note and replay the costumes I wear just in one day alone. Exhausting. Draining. Emotional. Hilariously wonderous. Does this resonate with you too?

If it wasn't for my ability to meditate, I wouldn't be able to detach and be objective. To witness this human self at play and not identify with the I form or beat myself up either. What's your favourite go to meditation? Mine is asking my mind to see with the eyes of love. Asking it further, what is the given gift? Then, after repeating this mantra several times until it is fully felt in the body, watching any 'negatively' charged thoughts dissolve into nothingness.

In this bit, I'd love to say that I am beyond grateful for all the wonderful people in my life right now, and to the ones who I haven't had the pleasure of meeting yet. Even Bill Gates … is he 100 per cent, truly trying to create a vaccine programme to de-populate humanity? Are we sleep walking into a black mirror hell reality? I wonder? What is a conspiracy theory and just who is telling the truth? Type it into Google, but be careful, one mis-leading or mis-spelt word and a potential ugly beast can rear its looming fangs and bite your ass. The origin of the word 'conspiracy' is Latin and means 'con' together and 'spiraire' we breathe. Does this sound like a malicious negative to you? Once, I absentmindedly typed into Google a documentary I was searching for about rare birds. Needless to say, I didn't get the feather variety but two birds and a one cup, porn kind. Of course, my curious mind started watching said film for a few curious moments until the poo scenes began oozing out. I'll leave the rest to your imagination. Totally vile, she says peeping through her fingers that are covering her eyes. Ever such a curious bunny. Tin hat removed.

I am thankful to all the men in my life too. I love them all, notice I don't use the word loved them all. I don't do past tense. The first love of my life, my Dad, and not my biological one because I wasn't meant to know him, but I'll talk more about him in my Darkness chapter later. Aren't all Dads little girls first boyfriends anyway?

To the handful of boyfriends, I had while growing up in my teenage tender years. I salute you. My nickname was 'The Fridge' at school. Wonder why? To my ex-husband, and my brother who sadly passed by suicide and my few boyfriends, and to my world, my son, I feel nothing but love. Another class song lyric by James.

Hooray to the women in my life, my lovely Mum Doris, my sisters, my cousins and nieces and Aunties and my chosen family. I love Elton John's new song named after that very sentiment, 'Chosen Family.' My Mum drilled this into me as a growing child that, 'blood wasn't thicker than water.' And how many years and tears did it take for me to really get this? And, to the woman who suffered so much sadness unable to keep me at birth. More on that in my Darkness Chapter also. Get your tissues ready. If you have been adopted too, you will identify with my downloaded pain.

Who have I missed out? Anyone? Visualise inserting a Ned Flanders finger roll in here. Ahhh, yes, there is someone....my precious ickle baba daughter. My amazing bundle of vivacious, fire cracking, thunderous life. You would have to meet her to understand why. I have no words, other than overflowing. Truly blessed that I am. Thanks Yoda voice. A mini me, strong willed, powerful, beautiful, and blessed as she is, sharing her many gifts with the world but unaware of a fuller potential yet. She's exactly where she is meant to be right now anyways, and doing fabulously so in her own right and why would I force anything else? There is always divine timing. I didn't have a clue about myself at 25 years and wasn't meant too. If someone forced me to wake up back then, I would have told them to fuck off too. The teacher presents itself when the student is ready for sure.

Beyond gratitude and love to you all. Much love and understanding in your universe.

In joy and enjoy the ramblings of a sightly crazy lady. Who incidentally, not in her wildest dreams, thought that she would become an Author, and write 2 books! Even if I was a gambling woman, I still never would have bet on that becoming true. Maybe I may write more? That's if you want me to.

My research and knowledge have come from many direct experiences, attending Tantra Retreats and Soul Level Workshops in Europe, India, and South America and from deep heart circle sharing's with other women. What is evident is that we all share heart-mind matters and creative sexual understandings at some point in time or other. We each suffer, the masculine too, often in silence, too afraid to share our innermost sacredness out of fear. As we have been conditioned to do so by our ancestors and their societal norms. I've spent the last 20 years, teaching, learning, and mentoring in Education, and the last 6 years studying my emotional landscape.

With many thanks to the universe of course, or the great mind, or higher consciousness, or source or God, or whichever term works best for you.

      Thank you. Enjoy the ride.
      It's nice to be nice.

Introduction

Who hasn't chased the holy grail of happiness?
However, when happiness arrives it seems so fragile and easily lost.
Ancient knowledge implies that happiness can be self-generated. The feeling of calm can be created in any moment, even amidst rush hour traffic or between a heated discussion with a loved one, and that kindness for ourselves and others can be consistent no matter what life throws at us.
Moreover, many gurus on social media instigate that we should all be experiencing this innate joy and feeling of abundance with upmost celebration and in totality because we have everything in front of us that we ever will need in the right here and now! If this is so, then why do we often perceive a feeling of lack?
It appears that this sense of 'lack' that we can sometimes feel in the present moment, can often reflect the care we received/perceived/downloaded into our memory file folder as a developing child, which gave us the imprint of 'lacking' in some way. This may show up in the 'how' we do something for ourselves in the now. With awareness, direct experience, knowledge, understanding and compassion, we can address any sense of lack by discovering new ways or helping techniques to nourish and nurture ourselves fully and truly. Drawing from my own experiences, it is not so much in the why but in the what we can do, that matters.

Drawing from my own experiences, I feel that to be more contented and present in life, the answers within us hold the keys to changing old predictable patterns of unwanted behaviours into new possibilities and new ways of living from our very own authentic, wild heart. To be better parents, improve our leadership skills and take ownership of our life and relating, to lead happier, and more fulfilled days. More living rich.

To be true, not in my wildest dreams did I ever envisage what would unfold for me in my lifetime. I sincerely did not see any of it coming. I am no psychic either but at the speed in which my life turned upside down and, on its head, intense is not the word. I wrote to my sister and told her of my impending hunch. That I've killed over 100 nuns in a former life. This is my dharma.

People often second guess their life mission, set linear goals, and have 5, or 10-year plans. I'm afraid mine is nothing like that. It was and is completely out of my non-linear hands and it seems the best thing I can do is write it all down as it occurs. Hint: Maybe this IS my life's mission? Behold! I can label myself an author! Drum roll please.

Incidentally, not since the release of my first book on 20th April 2021, during this transformative and historical pandemic, scamdemic, plandemic or whatever this containment period is or has been? Or what for? Did I know what would unfold for me. Did anyone for that matter? Although, this has been a gracious time for me and my beloveds. Heart wrenchingly so. You too, no doubt.

Indeed, for me, this 'lockdown' era has been a self-reflecting, trusting in the God opportunity. More so, it has given me the space to dive deeper into my spiritual heart and exercise all the understandings that I have been fortunate enough to discover. The 'God' label resonates for me for what you may call our higher source, intelligence, Christ Consciousness, or divine flow. But our God or just plain life if you like, can be brutal, rapid, soft, babbling, gentle, deep, azure blue, icy, glowing, shiny, radiating, stormy or calm. See how nature reflects us? Interchangeable, mysterious, and ever flowing?

For example, if there are rocks in the river, seemingly blocking the flow, the water will still find a way through the challenges. Just like us, we are solution bound. Always moving forward, never backwards. If God intended for us to go back, he would have designed us to walk backwards, yet our kinesiology is not set that way. We are fine tuned to drive forwards; this is our evolution. However, I do believe that reflection time spent does demonstrate kindness and compassion to our centre, our core being. Why? In learning how to reflect properly, it helps us to discover the lessons and blessings within our teachings in daily life. Often, with the best will in the world, you want to show more compassion and understanding to a fellow human, especially if they have pulled out in front of your car while riding a bicycle down a tight country lane, and you flipped the bird and honked your horn loudly in anger! Only to find out, in complete self-disgust, that on glancing in the mirror, this cyclist was an elderly woman, blowing out her backside, and really pushing it hard just to stay on her bike steering awkwardly uphill? Tut, tut.

Yet, life can happen so quickly, and with our current fast paced modern way of living, slowing down and smelling the roses, on a constant daily basis, is a tricky task to be or do. And, maybe, in that angry, reactive moment, that was a kind and compassionate state to be in, as that elderly cyclist needed that lesson. To give her an insight into something that life was telling her. You never can be too sure. Life will always and in all ways, my favourite mantra, deliver exactly what is needed at precisely the right moment. Aho, brothers and sisters. The teacher presents itself when the student is ready.

So why does the mind catastrophise for hours on end over stupid thoughts and give energy away to something that is not necessary? Something that used to keep me awake in bed at night and disturb my much-loved sleep. Here's were focused attention, mediation, or mindfulness kicks in. Learning to discern is vital. A wild hearted friend of mine once told me:

'That you have a heart that beats for you, lungs that breathe, a mind that thinks, but this is not you.'

Like it? I love it.

Let me also share briefly here why I refer to God as 'he.' I'm a visual person. God feels male to me, not in look but in a feeling way, but like a father's energy. It feels like something moving within and without, like a cool but firm breeze, but much more subtle than that. I really can't describe it as it is a deep knowing to me, that's all I can say about that, Forest Gump.

Talking about Forests. I'm sat here looking through my patio doors as I write, looking out at an awakening forest of bracken trees, just about to ignite into full foliage. I cannot live anywhere else other than deeply immersed in nature. It's my home, where I truly belong. There is so much wisdom in her intelligence, I refer to nature as her, why? Because she is everything to me, wild, soft, gentle, caressing, rugged, brutal, calming, energising and mystical. Just like a woman, cue Bob Dylan song, and 'she makes love like a little girl.'

In my world, God is a masculine energy and Nature is feminine and so very intertwined. This makes sense to me. I hope it does for you too.

Holey Moley.

We have God the Father and God the Son. Where is God the mother? God the daughter? God the sister? Where is "the Sacred Feminine" in our Judeo-Christian-Islamic Divine? Half the population of our world insists that the Divine has a gender, a word applicable solely in our limited reality. Why are the pulpit tyrants so anal?

Pope John Paul I, whose real name was Albino Luciani, was born 17 October 1912 and died on 28 September 1978, having spent about a month as Pope. Some say he was murdered.

Anyways, he was reported in the press as saying that we should see God not only as Father, but also as Mother. This remark strengthened the image of a pastoral pope.

Sadly, he died too soon. I wonder what he could have changed. I wonder if he got spent for saying God the mother. We kill cynics, don't we?

Speaking of love. We do not get love, we are love. How do I know this? Since the publication of my first book, it has taken me many years of self-discipline and self-enquiry to truly figure out my inner landscape? Remember in my first book in the final chapter how I stated, 'that I wanted to be a blondie? Making mistakes just like a little kid, building sandcastles and knocking them down again, re-emerging something new? Well, I've had a lot of fun times and painful ones too, the universe always must balance out our daily living to keep us all in homeostasis. Yet, in the process, I have found that I have had to let go of my old, conditioned beliefs. More so, I have a fuller awareness of the cheeky monkey mind (that inner dialogue in the head space) when those challenging thoughts pop up, but now I can watch them, more intimately, and then by following the breath, I have found out that they magically disappear! You must let go and get out your own way to receive your blessings to align with your highest truth. It is a tough skill set to truly master, which only deepens with on-going practice.

Voila!

This technique has helped me enormously in minimising most of my self-sabotaging behaviours or secondary gain projections that I have carried out unconsciously in the past. Trickily true.

Are you with me?

Furthermore, since writing my first book, Beyond Gratitude – A Journey to Positivity, it has taken me 6 gritty years to overcome my obstacles to unlock my future, ever evolving, human self, including shedding many tears, tantrums, warts, and all. To accept my imperfectly perfect self and feel inner ease. Plus, the continual unlocking of it as I have figured out that I am an endless, limitless form of bountiful possibilities, and that life is eternal. Until you pop your clogs and even then, I feel we change form to what the mind cannot comprehend. This has been no easy task either, let me assure you. Fucking really tough. I really do wonder how many nuns have I had killed in a previous life? I also think that reaching an end point of enlightenment like some schools of thought believe, is nigh on impossible. I do believe in enlightening light bulb moments though. Tad dah!

For sure, it has been a real self-mastery challenge to latch on to my limitless, to know how to heal my body, to develop and sustain heart, head, and gut coherence on a DAILY BASIS. And, yes, I had to write that in capitals as I am shouting this at you. You can't dip in and out of this like a pick and mix sweetie bag. Self-mastery is an every moment, of every waking hour, habitual way of living. Once you wake up, there is no going back, or playing at it. You are either in or out woke being. We are not a victim of our environment. We are the creators of it. Once you grasp that, that's it. Your awareness is razor sharp. You realise that other people cannot trigger you because if they did, you are reacting from a place in the past. Think of it in terms of having an old wound that has not been fully healed yet. Healing is like a spiral to me. We perceive that we have healed a wounded part of ourselves but then as we move further within, life presents us with another similar experience to make sure we have the lesson nailed. Believe you me, I have spent hours drawing out my adopted and biological parents timeline spiral dynamic to cross reference the simultaneous inter-dimensional, similar human behaviour, echoed in unison and parallel sequence. I hope that I have explained this to you as best I can, in my Northern ditsy, blondie versus silver crone streaks, twang.

Beyond more words.

Handy hack: In a moment of immediate challenge, learn how to self-correct, don't give your power away to that situation, instead, breathe into your present self and soften your body with a body scan. You cannot bypass any of this stuff.

What seems like many moons ago now, my chronic stress episode or 'awakening' that catapulted my healing heroines' journey around the globe, when life seemed like it was falling apart all around me, when in fact, it was falling back together just as it should be in any given moment. The reason for this is that it wasn't the monkey mind that was causing all the chaos, it was the inner dialogue in head trying to keep me safe as my risk manager. Nonetheless, it was my undigested monkey mind heart that was doing all the damage, and like a ball and chain, wrecking and destroying everything that I had and loved. It was all taken away from me. Completely tango. The upside was that from under the floorboards, I was slowly creating a newer version masterpiece of me. Although, I didn't know where to buy the canvas, paint, or paint brushes from at the beginning. I was too absorbed in my victim mentality. Also, the 'pain' I was feeling in my body was indescribably gut crunchingly intense. I really thought that I was going to die from the severity of my overwhelm and the dark thoughts that took me to places which frightened the pants off me.

How did I not know that I had grown into a repressed, oppressed, and supressed woman, who didn't feel safe in her own skin? How did I not recognise that my patterns and behaviours that I had learnt were coping mechanisms in response to my environment? How did I not realise in raising my own children that I was copying and pasting my learnt responses onto them? We have computer brains that copy and paste, copy and paste, copy and paste, copy and paste. Energy flows where energy goes.

Understanding that my wounded child from my adoption experience had downloaded a huge fear of abandonment. That adopted kids have an internal, no resting place and find it really hard to fully be seen by another in fear of? Yes, you've guessed it, being abandoned again. I now empathise with my adult self for the grief I felt at losing my parents within a few years of each other with undisclosed conversations that I will now never be able to have to understand them better. What did I only ever want? To feel wanted and needed at ALL costs. That is the Achilles heel that our Prime Creator stamped on me the day I entered the world, he didn't give me any dimples. Are you aware of yours?

That was an extremely tough life lesson and one of many.

I am now much better at letting go and fully trusting, even though I didn't want to at all. Yet, I wouldn't have had my first book published if I hadn't, nor would I have a clear voice and open heart to confidently share my insights with others. Knowing that I have connected and empowered just 1 other person in a meaningful way, makes my whole being glow. Nor would I have discovered the utter joy of cold-water dipping or the reignition of my passion for singing and freestyle shamanic tribal dancing or drumming. Oh, the joys of self-expression.

Moreover, I wouldn't dream of wishing what I went through on any other woman or family. It was truly traumatic for all involved. My intention through my words is to help you recognise your own limitations and thus, reclaim your expression. Locate a group of like-minded others with whom you feel safe with to develop a trusting relationship so that you explore, at your own pace, your challenges. Seek professional help, try many forms until you feel that you have a resonance to move forward in your life, to create the vision of you that is also seeking you. If you don't succeed with a match initially, keep going until you do. Compassionately dissolve the onion layers in your own unique, authentic way. I love the term de-armouring one-self! The spiritual teacher,

Jeff Foster talks about this a lot. We are all unique and exquisite flowers in this garden we call life. One size does not fit all.

The feminine way is the way of softness, gift yourself deep embodiment practices to ground the opening of your heart that happens when you truly give yourself permission to blossom, at your own unique pace, in your own exclusive way. That is the way of the feminine. We have challenged our masculine counterparts, equalling their butchness for way too long now. It's old hat. The time has come for a new approach, to use our feminine essence as our God intended, to meet and merge with our masculine complements to assist in the creation of our new world. A loving and peaceful one that is emerging ultimately. The patriarchal way has held the reins for too long now. Our women have suffered enough. It's time to make a united stand, hand in hand we all stand together, boom, boom. Thank you, Paul McCartney, even the frog song held valuable insights as they have been singing about this for years!

Know this. Woman, I love you for everything you have experienced and endured, and your ancestors' ancestors too. I am with you in this collective pain. Sisters, I hear you and feel it all. I love you some more.

My intention as I write is always pure. Nothing but love. The dear people that I talk about in this narrative, I love you too, and there is absolutely no malicious intent in my sharing these words. I struggle to find the right words sometimes because my ocean is deep. My deepest desire is that you will find some comfort in my words, and that in some way, it helps you with something that is going on within you on a deeper level. Everything is an inside job.

The way out is the way in.

Totally everything. How we feel, how we think, how we act, how we communicate, how we see, how we make love, and what we want to create, are all driven from within. As within, so without. By the way, we do have to make love, it is an act of divine bliss, not a fuck, quick act, release me love. Not that I'm dissing quickies here, if the consensual intention is clean and clear, an animalistic, passionate exchange can be cosmic. Everything is intention. You know that saying, attention flows where energy goes. Winkey face. More on my views on sex later.

I will talk more about the monkey mind heart, giving you more detail later in this book. But for now, I just want you to know that I have come to a place of relaxation with my former strict practices. I have found great comfort in the safety and science of my self-help toolkit that has helped me enormously thus far. Involving a daily dose of self-loving rituals, including a diet of soul nourishing, life giving, food, regular movement, followed by various models of meditation, and enjoying sensual touch, taking wild dips in icy cold rivers, and playing musical instruments and singing again. Even the odd glass of wine or two!

Maybe, it is because I have hit half a century and have successfully overcome my peri-menopausal years finally? Or that I have reached a daringly selfish point in my life, when my body mind knows exactly what it needs for nourishment and to feel alive. In a feminine flow manner.

I do not know. Other than right now, as I share my musings, I'm enjoying a slice of homemade gooey vanilla cheesecake and grapefruit tea. Delicious. And I thank this for nourishing every little cell in my body.

However, I certainly do feel more peaceful, benevolent, and less reactive. I feel that my primal screaming sessions up on the moors has alleviated a lot of my pent-up anger. Instead, now flowing with life, like a river, wild and carefree, flowing with abundance and living the dream. Nice singing lyrics those. Imagine the sound of harmonised voices while taking a cold dip up in the hills? Imagine this; harmonious earth angels collectively singing from the heart in the wild open waters, bathing safely together, honouring our differences, expressing as we each individually must? Some bathing in their birthday suit, shinning their glorious pubic hairy mounds upon the sunlight, others partially clothed. Point being that there is no judgement either way, as full respect for another's level of resting in their comfort and safety zone is paramount. Second point. Of all the sacred elements, water must be the most mysterious and feminine. The shape shifter, the fog, ice, steam, frost, snow, hail, rain, droplets, and deep, vast ocean. Water dances in and around us, the sacred spirit water element.

Incidentally, there is no talk of trauma, but each heart can feel a deep rawness and a letting go in those mystical and magical sacred waters. Listen for long enough and you will hear Mother Nature's voice communing with you too. Can you be quiet enough for long enough to hear her whispers? Can you feel the love of Mother Earth under your sodden souls and connect to the currency of gratitude?

Priceless.

At last, my natural rhythm of life has been found. I sleep very well, like a bear, every night. I wake with the singing birds; I move my body as and how she wants to each day. Is this selfish? I am my number one priority. I even love my wobbly belly and squidgy thighs. Can you stand Infront of a full-length mirror full on and honestly not criticise any part of your body for working for you? Do you send out positive vibes to yours? Do you craft time out each day to honour your needs? Are you selfish enough?

In daylight, can you look at your full-length naked body in the mirror, and say with full reverence,' YOUR NAME, I LOVE YOU.' Perhaps, you can even celebrate further by throwing a wiggle or a jig too?

For me, that is the penultimate self-love, real assessment.

If I cannot fulfil my own needs first, then how on earth can I ever meet the needs of any beloved others fully? It's just not possible and not in alignment with my highest value, which is me. And by the way, if you haven't come across Dr John DeMartini's work yet, then do look him up. He's a rather special chap with copious amounts of divine wisdom and intelligence. Part of me feels that he talks from his cognitive head a lot, as he has absorbed so many books with his photographic mind, and I cannot feel his heart in totality. Although he does have one or he wouldn't do or be who he scholarly is.

This is what I've learnt, from experience, and not through a textbook. That one person cannot be our everything and all, yet, our conditioning promotes a partnership marriage for life. The co-dependant destructive type. What if from any early age we discovered the beauty in all human beings and that each unique person has a wonderful gift within them to share like a stitch within this tapestry called life? What if we were solid in this knowledge, and I don't mean from a head perspective, I mean an embodied one. That, in essence, we gave ourselves permission to co-exist in community with others, interdependently, beautifully, so kind, and compassionate to our own needs initially, reflecting theirs? Why have we been taught to cling in misery because our significant other is lacking in some way? That he doesn't do this, or he/she doesn't do that. What if we started accepting and celebrating what they do do instead? Why not come to a place of acceptance and understanding that that is what they have been shown too? What if they can't put a nail in the wall because their father didn't show them or wasn't interested? What if their highest value isn't DIY, it's yours, but you can't own it? What if your significant other just adores reading and they just buzz off the idea of spending hours dreamily browsing in bookstores? Much to your distaste. More so, that this very fact could cause an explosive reaction and negatively charged response. Whatever happened to acceptance? I water you; you water me.

Currently, there are so many books out there on relationships, on building resilience and maintaining heart coherence which I love. In particular, I am a big advocate of HeartMath and their simple awareness techniques. I'm not sure about the heart monitor, I'm not a gadget person, I'm a minimalist, and hate clutter. Plus, I have a heart and pulse, I don't need to see it on a PC screen to know how my body feels. I can close my eyes and do that, then self-regulate accordingly to that present moment and act accordingly. This is the thing that I've also discovered, emotional self-regulation does not follow a set pattern. It ebbs and flows just like the waters in my beloved rivers. There is no one size fits all, a set routine or performance. It's about being fully right here and now in the present moment and breathing deeply right into that and deeply knowing from within the body, how and where it is speaking to you from, and then following that. That is what I've come to know as honouring yourself, listening to your truth, giving yourself permission to tell a trusted other exactly what you need, even if it means a charged reaction from them, maybe they are not ready? The trick here is using what I call Clean Talk Communication, you need to speak slowly and clearly with a neutral tone and speak directly into the essence of life. If you do this, watch what magically happens next.

I kid you not, it's a great technique, but sorry forgot to add, if only used in full awareness of the moment and with the highest intention of love and trust. Brené Brown uses a technique called 'circling back,' but there is no back in my world, I use, in each challenging moment, a version called 'circling up and out,' much more appropriate don't you agree?

Incidentally, have you heard about HeartMath? They have conducted scientific experiments to measure the emotional distance or range at which a heart can feel or sense energy from? Guess what? It is exactly 2 metres.

Two metres apart.

Has that got you thinking? Have you ever been in a crowded room and felt your eyes drift across the room to someone who has tugged at your heart strings without acknowledging them first? That is your hearts intelligence. Same sense you get when you are driving in your car, and you sense that you are being looked at. Your eyes follow your heart's deeper sensing. Different scenario but same response.

That is the magic of the heart.

Here is a little ditty that I jotted down.

Life is a dance,
Two left feet,
Bruised toes,
An unforgettable high,
For a short time,
Crescendo halts,
Bodies abrupt,
To turn and part to another partner,
For another dose of two left feet and bruised toes.

Just a thought. But what if we celebrated divorce with a parting of ways? Giving thanks for the relating and experiences shared? What if this was a whole family occasion? No dogma, just tears of joy and knowing gratitude? What if the relatives stayed in touch and offered support when needed? Why does a family go through a breakdown when life has other ideas in store? I cannot work this out. Obviously, its years of conditioning. However, on another note, how beautiful if our world lived in co-creation, of shared expression? As opposed to suppression, oppression or repression?

I am a typical Libran who loves all things bright and beautiful just like the song, in balance and harmony. Yet, I do know the contrast, there is always the dark. I will tell you more about my experiences in the dark later on. EEK, be warned, these experiences are not for the faint hearted! You may need to lie down in a dark room for a very long time afterwards. Not in a horror movie scary Scream kind of way. Although, if your life experiences are anything like mine and you are a super sensitive being, then maybe you will know exactly what I will discuss from your own viewpoint.

If you prefer an authentic read to digest, something to stimulate the senses and capture the imagination over a coffee? Minus gimmicks? Read on. This book is for you my lovely friend.

Why waste any more precious time on yet another unwanted, so-called informative, healing Blog post. Another load of dribble trying to permeate the mind, trying to get your email subscription, buy

an online course, get this, or that, or the other which you are not remotely interested in.
One-Click-and boom, it vanishes, into the spam folder vortex of junk.

Me too. I do not want to be fixed or rescued. I am not broken, nor do I desire advice or other projections! I am perfectly whole as I am. There is no such thing as good advice either!

Of course, having worked as a schoolteacher for decades I am aware of the astute English language structure and of its enticing benefits. Over the years I have helped many carefully utilise alliteration, metaphors, quirky opening statements, snappy slogans, and other such language skill sets to engage and excite a reader and make that transaction!

However, do you feel drained and completely bored with the tyranny of it all? For me, it's like walking down the high street and noticing 10 Starbucks coffee shops, one after another, after another. Offering no authenticity, uniqueness, individuality, humour, inspiration; just a flatter than flat, flat as a pancake flat, boring white.

Why is this so?

We are conditioned and brainwashed to vote with mind. Live in the mind, talk and believe everything the mind has taught so far. Well, why not? It has been a safe, reliable friend for so long.

Still, are you a feeling lost in the world?

Let's be clear it is not your fault. We are programmed by society to feel this way. The more you have, the more you fear losing it, a drain to anyone's soul!

This read is an invitation to come out of the head and into the heart space of feeling. An invitation to allow the intelligence of the heart to guide you, which in fact it can if you ponder over the research carried out at HeartMath to live your wildest dreams. Do you desire to live peacefully, and treat yourself gently? Are you willing to allow life to flow through you each day, employing mindful and conscious choices? Most people walk around all day completely unconscious of their choices, or are aware of cause and reaction or wonder why things keep showing up for them?

Our lives are complex, busy, and stressful, with too many things to do, too many conflicting responsibilities, too many possessions and too little time. This can leave us feeling overwhelmed, disconnected, and burnt out. Our consumerist society encourages a mindset of wanting more and wanting things quickly.

Practices such as Meditation or Mindfulness (as known in the Western society today) have been developed over centuries to support us in opening to the beauty and discernment of a simpler life. They can transform our own lives and the world.

Developing patient, loving awareness can help you slow down and open to the pleasure of being present with yourself and with life. It helps cultivate gratitude and appreciation for where you are and what you have

This is not about self-denial but instead a fuller experience of what we already have. In embracing simplicity, we have the potential to make our lives richer, more beautiful and to focus on what really matters. Simplicity is not about giving up the positive benefits of modern life, but rather making more careful choices about our lifestyles and actions. These effects have a positive impact on the environment, helping us to tread more lightly on the earth.

To really embrace simplicity, we need to be sensitive to our inner world, to meet any feelings or emotions with kindness, understanding and courage.

Do you choose to embrace simplicity through each encounter and feel more alive, more in touch with what matters and more truly able to live in harmony with ourselves, and others, both near and far, and with the earth itself? Or do you choose to overindulge in wheat, sugar, alcohol, nicotine or drugs, porn or gambling or similar distractive devices to push down your inner world of fear and confusion and as a substitute for love?

So what?

This is ok too.

If my words resonate with you on what my beliefs on how this thing called life really works, ask yourself, how deeply do you connect to others without judgments?

Essentially, humans experience parallel emotions and traumatic life experiences which impacts our families, societies, and community etc., We are the same and should value each other more than we do.

Are you sick and tired of feeling sick and tired of disconnection from others? Would you like to drop your mask? Are you courageous enough to expose your beautiful vulnerability? Do you have the resolve to explore your lurking shadow story? Are you willing to start listening to the intelligence of your heart, and become so fully present with the whole of you're being, so that this thing called life starts to become peaceful, joyful, and simpler for you?

People often make the mistake of burying their unresolved childhood memories under the carpet of compassion, even if your parent(s) did their best. It doesn't mean that you don't have a right to your own healing journey. For me, we do not heal from trauma, we find ourselves in it. We break the cycle once we turn our compassionate eye internally, nurturing our own inner wounds as best we can.

We could be more sensitive to our inner world, to meet any feelings or emotions with kindness, understanding and courage. Thankfully, Meditation practice taught me how to transform the mind with satisfying reflection, with the ability to listen to my heart, allowing me to naturally shift towards contentment, connection, and beautiful simplicity.

It is important to understand that we are human beings, not human doings, we are energetical, vibrational, super amazing vehicles of consciousness, engineered master pieces, works of art that has the capacity to remarkably feel into the feeling frequencies of others too.

Many people think that practice of spirituality is a dogma, cult, or religion but it is merely a way of loving all the self, very deeply, in total presence or simply put in touch with our spirit.

For example, sadly, Islam has been once again in the media; blamed for the acts of terror in Manchester and our capital city.

However, the true message of any faith; be it Christianity, Islam, or Buddhism etc., is about compassion, peace, and love. Therefore, an act of terror cannot validate a true definition of one's faith. How can it?

The prayer of Saint Francis says it all:

"Lord, make me an instrument of Your peace. Where there is hatred, let me sow love; where there is injury, pardon; where there is doubt, faith; where there is despair, hope; where there is darkness, light; where there is sadness, joy.
O, Divine Master, grant that I may not so much seek to be consoled as to console; to be understood as to understand; to be loved as to love; For it is in giving that we receive; it is in pardoning that we are pardoned; it is in dying that we are born again to eternal life."

My heart goes out to all those suffering within.

Is it necessary to participate in this collective frantic fear? Feeling our own natural fears as they arise through living is beautifully scary enough and takes enormous amounts of courage.

Fundamentally, at the deepest level, it is the natural, authentic state of being, present and powerful in every moment by moment which is truth, as we learn to relax more. This is my truth. However, this is only my interpretation, rather than the objective truth, please remain aware.

Oh, what a magical gift to be able to alter our perceptions of life and subsequently our approach to each day as we jump out of bed and breathe, yes breathe. There are so many people who sadly experience breathing difficulties and need specialist breathing equipment, or those who don't make it through the night as their last breath is stolen, just like my dear beloved Mother.

Oh, the joys of the breath! Oh, the simplicity of life!
Have you ever woken up in the morning and simply thanked your breath for just breathing life into you? Even whilst you slept soundly.

Do you still feel, 'So what?'

Truth

What does this word mean exactly? The Oxford Dictionary defines this word as 'the quality or state of being true.'

What does this word mean to you?

How does this word and meaning affect the way that you live your life?

On one occasion I remember, as a double figure cheeky teenager, my Mum forcing me to put my right hand down on the Bible to swear on, to prove that I was telling the truth. I can't remember what big, fat, whopping lie I told, but I knowingly waited for my karma to be served. Still, it was a better option than being force fed a box of cigarettes to eat, which one of my friends strained to do once. Oh, and I remember another friend had to gargle with a dollop of gloopy washing up liquid for her bad behaviour. So, I think I got off pretty lightly considering. Even though they are all technically fucked up punishments, yet no target was scarred for life. Were you?

Roses are red,
Violets are blue,
I'm a schizophrenic,
So am I.

Joking!

Back in those days, the option of threatening your parents by calling Childline didn't exist. Not even when your Dad took his belt off and cracked it together with both ends, to assume a whack across the arse. Kids in the 70's and 80's didn't answer back, swear in front of their parents, ate the food they were given, and went to bed when they were told. Elders were respected, and Sunday was a respected day, in leisurely slowness including sharing the traditional roast dinner which was a typical family occasion. This one meal time, I fondly remember trying to get my younger brothers and sisters in trouble for laughing at me behind my parents back, while gurning my mashed potato up in my mouth and pretending to dribble it off my tongue. Grosse.

Incidentally, when did the Tikka Masala become the UK's number one Sunday meal?

Also, my Dad would stand there for hours in front of the TV, proudly ironing all 4 school uniforms, and diligently polishing four pairs of shiny shoes. He spent many years in the Army, and I was fascinated by how he would fervently spit and polish those sets of shoes up, ready for our week ahead in school. He was an Army Veteran. I was so proud of him. Acts of love. I didn't recognise it at the time. How could I? He reminded me of the story of The Elves and Shoemaker, my proud Dad did.

Nonetheless, I was a kid and meant to be selfish as fuck. I thought all the practical chores my parents did were just to keep us clothed, fed, and watered. How wrong. They don't teach you about that in school, do they? I've never heard any dialogue before. Not in my twenty years in education anyway. So, Mum and Dad wherever you are in your universe, I love you to the moon and back and I know that no apology is needed because you did the best job ever and you knew, without words, moral values, and the cycles of child development. I never got to tell you in person that you are my heroes.

I'm owning this too, when my Mum crashed and bombed out on the sofa after her stint at work for a much-needed rest, did I understand why during my tender years? She walked to and forth for an hour each day to her part time job, plus stayed on top of all housework and upkeep of our home, and with four extremely lively characters to pertain. Not to mention that she made the best roast dinner with mushy peas. Crikey, I really did think she was Superhuman, my Dad too, they both seemed to be possessed with phenomenal powers.

This one time, after what must have been a tough day at work for her, I vividly remember her telling me that she was 'not asleep but resting her eyes,' when she was apparently knackered and obviously dealing with an inner struggle. That's unconditional love for you, over and beyond. That was my Mum, never complaining and always powering forward with her warrior energy. Pesky sod I was.

Like most children, I didn't think of them as humans, who would eventually leave us. Well, in body form at least. I thought they would live forever. What a reality shock I got when they passed. The lead balloon type. Resurfacing my abandonment trauma, type wound, BIG TIME.

So, my truth and not the absolute, is this, as I now settle into my maturing 50+ years, I can honestly and sincerely say because I feel that at last, I am at home in my own skin. Despite both my parents passing, a divorce, and waking up to the knowledge that my kids belong to life and are happily creating their own fun realities. For I have I too, managed to relinquish my 'empty nest syndrome.' Something I first noted when they became teenagers, eagerly venturing out into the unknown and excitedly began exploring and leaving the nest. Cutting those apron strings has been tricky, alongside a pesky perimenopause. Painfully so at times.

Thankfully, that part of me has also melted into understanding and total joy when they call me to tell new something new or to teach me something about their day. I'm thrilled.

Feeling at home in your own skin, as some call being embodied, has taken me rather a few years to master, that and time alone to excavate my inner world of traumatising experiences which my body has held onto fervently (I'm loving this word currently).

When I mention trauma, this is a word which triggers most of us, but I cannot think of another softer word for the darker experiences that, as a growing human, we all experience in childhood, and yet, it is these very experiences that shape us in later life. If we learn how to properly understand this, that is. What I'm really trying to say here, is that our childhood wounds are not who we are. They are part of our story stored in our unconscious mind bodies. The trick in life is to know that recovery does not come from outside of you, from materialistic sources, but from within you. From self-reflection, enquiry and deep, honest, and open conversations with yourself and daily rituals that serve you. It does not come from Netflix, a new handbag, Botox or new house, a baby etc. Otherwise, you will you distracting yourself even more from what wants looking at. Take courage my friend, seek out those who have the skilled knowledge and proficiencies to assist you on your journey. To make the unconscious drivers conscious. Don't wait like I did for a catastrophe to happen. It seems like most people wake up when dealt the pain card. Why wait?

Trauma is trauma and if there were a circle of sharing others and one mentions a rape and another mentions not being breast fed or being bottle fed properly, or another mentions a beating, or being locked away in their room for hours on end, left to cry. Do you think we have a trauma gauge that states which one is the worst experience? Does this sound kind? Well, can you distinguish which is the most horrifically traumatising experience and claim that it requires more nourishment and healing and attention? Do you hear how heartless that sounds?

Ridiculous? It does to me.

We already have an autistic spectrum, why create any unethical others?

Any traumatic experience is just that, trauma is trauma, and it's left residing in the body, in the facia, in the sinews, in the muscle memory, in every conceivable cell. For me, no amount of any type of talking therapy will ever be sufficient to heal those wounds. The Body Keeps the Score, read Bessel Van Der Kolks work, he will articulate more. I know from my own journey that the body needs to move, it needs to release, it needs to be witnessed by a significantly qualified, and experienced professional other, who can deeply hold space and take accountability for such a catalytic and momentous recovery, without, incidentally, allowing the healing experience to energetically impinge on their situation. They must know how to energetically protect themselves. In a nutshell, what I mean is, that it does not affect their sleeping patterns, it does not go over and over in their mind, that it essentially does not affect them or interfere with their daily life or absorb them. Otherwise, they just haven't done the work needed to truly assist another in letting go and healing. I've expressed that as simply as I could, I hope it makes sense to you. Trauma cannot be seen with the psychical eye. It is subtle, felt and repaired with love. It's an energy and only love is the answer to recover those fragmented parts of self.

So, you see, this is immensely tricky work. A lot of it is on the subtle level, but it is possible and can be cleaned and cleared. This I know for sure from my own direct experiences in life. For me, it's all about getting the body moving in which way resonates with everyone on an individual level. It is not set in stone, for we are not robotic morons, we each have a unique DNA gene code that requires specific modalities which will resonate at the deeper level. Some love primal screaming, some love smashing plates, some will love massage, some will love singing, some will love dancing, or yoga. Some people will love to be left alone in quiet times, or to go for a run, cycle, or wild swim. Some will love the cold, other people the heat. Others will require a sensual yoni or lingam massage; some may just love skin on skin and only want their neck to be intimately touched. The semantics of somatic. Pain in the neck anyone?

With the correct intention, and witness, and time and patience you can become your own self master and healer. Ask your body what it needs to heal? Learn how to deeply listen to the wisdom it holds. Discover how to have a dialogue with those body parts that are talking to you, giving you the information as to what wants healing. Take as much time as you need. There is no rush, Rome wasn't built in a day. What do you desire? What are your dreams? Can you communicate your sentiments properly and without restriction? Is your throat centre open for natural discourse? Can you be still and quiet enough to listen in? Can you hear the calling of your inner guru, your intuitive wisdom? Can you follow through with the necessary healing action?

The middle age years of a woman's life are formative. They cannot be taken for granted or allowed to pass by in a sea of struggle, stress, and sacrifice. My life's direction in my forties were a complete nightmare. Classic case of mid-life crisis, or mid-life transformation or just simply seeking change due to chronic stress. What I do know is this, the former Sarah had checked out. She was overweight, boozy, toxic, and inflamed and a walking dumping ground. Call it what you will, but it was cathartic as hell. I wouldn't wish it on anybody. If I can support just one other person with my words, then my life has been worthwhile.

Can you imagine my conversation with a conventional GP? I was given long term prescription drugs for depression and beta-blockers to slow my heart down and numb down my anxiety and depression. Did I tell the GP of my drinking habit? To stuff down my emotions and self-sabotage. Did I tell her of my mystical experiences? My outer body and disturbing involvements? What do you think?

As per, I picked the medication up from the pharmacy, took them all diligently, well why would I not? I did not know of anything else at the time. Then what happened? Mixed with the alcohol, I began shutting down even further. My ex-husbands mantra, 'go to the doctors and get help,' that was his limiting belief and the one that I fell for and knew all too well myself. I knew no other way. My mindset was very closed. Understanding how sickness manifests in the body does take some serious research time on, and a deep-down core belief to know this to be true.

Thank God my adult children have seen the light now and do talk with me as much as they can, and not because they feel sorry for a crazy lady but because they want to. To be fair, I converse with my son more than my daughter right now, but more on that later. Thank God too that my ex-husband has now found love again. He deserves it immensely; he has the heart the size of Mars, but our paths hit the crossroads crisis of choosing growth or stuck sameness. Thankfully, he's swanking it up on the red carpet with his new beau, and that's exactly where he should be. He said to me once in the kitchen during our departing that I never loved him. Fool. I was tongue tied in my head; I'd never given myself permission to speak. I'd loved him dearly for so many years and for so many memories, simply put, I just didn't love myself or understand myself in any way. Not socially, emotionally, spiritually, or mentally. I was highly unaware in those departments. How can you love another when your own beating heart does not love itself? I was internally frozen and lost because I had never figured out my trauma patterning or conditioning or made sense of any of it. In true Great British style, I soldiered on and kept a stiff upper lip.

I do wish that there was a book out there to prepare you for these, and it seems, ten yearly cycles. And I don't mean a book written by some airy-fairy floss head, who projects that she's got all her shit together raising the perfect family with her perfect Botox fillers and gleaming turkey teeth. I mean penned by a cool, wholesome bitch who I would have resonated with, and not the performance variety. A woman who is free to make her own statement about who she is in totality, chin whiskers, hairy legs, and all. Probably one of the reasons why I hated social media when it first came out on the scene. I really did believe that everyone was honest and authentic who posted meticulously on there. I soon coined the term 'mask disorder.'

Well, that's what I did and had expectations of the same. My awakening years were insane, were insane in the membrane and reality, I questioned.

Over the years, did I realise that this cyber beast has created a serpent snake of ambiguity. I believe that there are psychological concerns that we do not have a label for just yet, but I do feel that social media has created a diverse reality and personas. One for the camera, one for living reality. The one on social media is artificial with clever hacks to draw you in, unconsciously and often consciously. It's a dynamic two headed serpent. One the one hand there is psychological disidentification, and on the other there also a lot of positivity. However, is it always possible to discern which one is helpful or unkind? Can you imagine the conversations needed with young spongey growing mind? Or is it easier for adult or carers to simply adjust their security settings? How do you begin these conversations? At what level? I grew up painting clay, with my gold nail varnish, that I had dug up from the garden and tried to flog. Kids today are scrolling, eyes glued to a screen at 3. I witness this daily in restaurants and being pushed in prams. Do you notice this creeping normalised trend?

For me, until I taught vulnerable kids in care, labelled as having Social Emotional Mental Health concerns, did I come to know the extent of self-harming platforms and the tribal identity created with that. No, it isn't trendy, the more you cut yourself doesn't deem you cool. You are suffering and in need of copious amounts of love and support. Likewise, to the ones suffering with body dysmorphia. I love you too. Shame but in the DSM-5 diagnostic and statistical manual of mental health disorders medical journal, currently there are 300 mental health concerns. I wonder how many more there will be in the next ten years. I wonder what professional bodies will label traumatised teenagers as, who angrily self-stimulate or shove artefacts into their sexual organs, or inflict serious self-harm because they have survived being drugged and micro-chipped for the child sex industry? Or the ones who bark like a dog on all fours on top of a table who have experienced a feral upbringing devoid of human contact? Or the ones who have been gang raped by paedophile rings? Or the ones who have been lifted off the streets as drug mules? Or had their arms broken to sell drugs in the ever-growing county lines culture? Or the ones who have been only fed ketchup as a food staple? All shockingly true realities.

For certain, Life is a rollercoaster, Ronan Keating, and challenging at times, and authentic role models who speak the truth and who are fully transparent, are much needed right now in all nations. How can the Kardashians cut the mustard? Come on, its reality TV, they live a game show lifestyle. Who rocks up to the supermarket wearing rubber pants and 6-inch platforms with a face that could be chiselled it's that cacked in make-up and loaded with fillers, it's a lizard mask! Of the brief times I've encountered them on TV, I presumed I was watching a rocky horror show. Dare you reveal your true selves, pimples, and all, wearing your best beige Bridget Jones pants.

That's why I love the English comedian Sarah Millican, she's that boringly normal she's hilarious! I can imagine her being the same in real life as she on TV. I bet she has period knickers and has a penchant for socks and sandal wearing too.

To conclude, and going off on a teacher tangent, but this is my prerogative Bobby Brown, Truth is authentic living, devoid of self-sabotaging, destructive tendencies, it is pure awareness and wholehearted living in joy and positivity, creating as God designed, in kindness and compassion for the number 1 self. Just like Princess sings with heart and soul, 'say I'm your number 1.' Love thyself first, causes loving ripple effects to others. Simple. You don't have to be no Einstein to work that one out.

This is my final say on stripping back, of peeling back the onion layers of limiting beliefs and old conditioning paradigms. To add, a dear friend of mine has been doing this work for over 20 years now. Longer than a life sentence in prison! Stripping back and doing the graft, repeatedly to clean and clear her deeply embedded trauma. Bless her, she's now found her gold and is living it. I am blessed to know her and mention that, despite her challenging, traumatic, tender developing years, she has come to recognise that her trauma does not hold her any longer, she holds it. My love, there is only the present moment just breathe and be now.

You are the container, not the contained. You do not heal from trauma,
You find healing 'in' the trauma.

Jeff Foster

Dear friend if this sounds like you too, trust me, life does get easier in time, with kindness, forgiveness, and gentleness and forming trusted bonds with like-minded others. It is the way of the feminine. Although, it's a lengthy process like unravelling a ball of tangled wool. For me, it's finding a balance between holding on and letting go, to surrender and receive what is, in the absolute divine timing of the universe. Eeek. Hold on to your knickers darling. Why spend longer than a custodial sentence suffering?

What is time exactly? If there only is the present moment, could it be argued that the body ages and decays to reflect this thing we call time? Giving us an indication of a passing of something? In the now, now, now, and now?

Incidentally, as a wild dipper and advocate of cold water and the whisperings that this medicine brings. I'm going to live until I'm a 100 and still look 15 years old. Funny story is, that I have recently been asked for ID when purchasing wine!

Thank you for reading thus far and hearing my truth. I will again state this this is my truth alone, not the absolute. This is what is missing to many nowadays, the ability to fully share what is within the heart space with another, without discernment, to be heard and seen. Then, and only after that, could we come to a democratic solution to move forward.

Two key skills for growth. Active questioning and solution focused resolution.

I do not see enough people these days who ask the right questions, or any for that matter. Only choosing to accept what is presented. I call these type of people sheepeople. I ask myself, is this out of fear or lack of education? Or a fear of being triggered and not knowing what to do about it?

Tell me why?

Is it now safer and has become more acceptable to write on a friend's 'wall' rather than speak in real time? Have we really become a nation of electronic communicators and lost the real art of empathic interaction? Has this containment period wiped out all our social skills for good? When did airing your social grievances for a like become the norm? My Mum never put her dirty laundry out on the washing line for all the neighbours to see. Is there no such thing as privacy anymore? Why do I need to know that you have had pizza last night for your tea? Who cares if your oven has exploded, or your car has a flat tyre? Or that you have a parking fine. No one cares. As for virtual hugs. No thank you. Only the real McCoy will do to raise my vibration. Salt and Vinegar flavour for me please. Grab bag size.

For our future generations, we must begin to tap into this methodology of non-reactive questioning and informative decision making for us to sustain a brighter world. Neglect COVID 19, for me climate change, starvation and impending wars take priority. If we each did our bit, there will be a world ahead waiting for us all. No wonder Elon Musk, the Tesla boss wants to buy and is interested in (or has bought by now) an island somewhere in Indonesia (Biak, I think) and plans to completely flatten it to potentially launch SpaceX rockets up in space missions to create new, other worlds outside earth. Can you see why? If we don't get a handle, Mother Earth and Father Sky could hit that self-destruct button. Musk is a visionary. Ask Google. But, at the price of what exactly? The loss of local traditions and cultures, communities, families, plus wildlife, this could be devasting annihilation against many principles and beautiful peoples.

Our Grandfathers would never have predicted that in ten years' time it will be possible to mine on Mars. Scientists have discovered minerals that our precious Mother Earth needs. How mind bending is that?

Lastly, I will mention our current prime minister, Boris Johnson. I cannot resist. It is my book after all, and my heart mind gives itself permission to speak my truth. Right now, we still have freedom of speech, yet God knows how many underhanded policies have been slipped through under the guise of COVID. Whatever happened to democratic parliamentary debates? I fondly enjoyed those! Boring though they may have appeared. I have, only 2 rules in my life ...

Don't watch the News and stay off the scales.

Consequently, our Great British empire demands fresh, wholesome meat, and vital role models as leaders. Not the boarding school screwed up out of touch with reality variety. The kinder, earthier sort. When I tune into my heart and gut brains intelligence and enquire if BJ demonstrates trusting leadership skills, I must honestly answer no. My rational? It's very simple. I am feminine, and just look at how many children he has? At least 6 that he knows about. Perhaps there's a few more that he isn't aware of either? If this good for our climate, for our eco footprint, for the environment? Is having such a large family a good thing for the public to witness? Aspire to? Ever thought about just how many nappies, pairs of shoes, food etc, heating, etc etc., just one child needs growing into adulthood on this planet? Watch David Attenborough's, 'Our Planet' and with immediate sadness see how our wildlife and green spaces have diminished over the years, then with anticipated belief that if we all ACT accordingly now, then all is not lost. Watch also, 2040 on Amazon Prime, our world has the potential to be incredible if we open the door to say yes to building connections and not possessions. I am not a fantasist either, I'm a positive realist. I'm earth, air, fire, and water. I'm all the elements intertwined.

Shake, shake, shake, shake, shake, shake, your booty.

Ditch and BAN all plastic water bottles too. Interestingly, I never knew what a plastic water bottle was a kid. I drank milk from a paper carton in school and water from the tap. I've lost count of the number of horrific sea creatures that have been forced to ingest this deadly toxic junk. Funnily, folk talk of being 'green or eco-friendly,' I feel we were far more of both in my younger years. We drank pop from a glass bottle which was recycled and refilled, my siblings and I would excitedly argue for the 20p to scoff penny sweets from the local sweet shop. We had just 1 TV in the whole house, and we walked everywhere when we were little as my parents couldn't afford a car. Not many people did in those days. Also, clothes were handed down. It was an honour to get clothes from one of your much-loved friends or cousins. Even if it didn't fit properly, you still felt as though you were cool.

Incidentally, I'm not advocating a 1 child policy like in China, even though this is no longer in force, and it did produce some very powerful women! But I do think that as a nation we are moving away from enabling the fact that no longer can we tolerate single mothers or low paid couples churning out a child each year to pay for their council homes and claim benefits? I have worked in low social status demographics. I've known the hacks and games people play to 'beat' the system as the system is beating them. I've known a single parent who birthed 9 children! Yes, 9! I'm no politician but what I do know is that we need to find another way. Of inclusion, self-support, and contribution. Research the 6 elements Tony Robbins bangs on about, what every human design needs to feel to evolve healthily; certainty, uncertainty, significance, and contribution but without connection or love, there is no spiritual growth.

At least Prince Harry and Meghan have spiritual sense, in declaring that they will only have two children in their partnership to do their bit for the eco climate. How refreshingly wonderful, unlike his brother and his Mrs who seem be popping them out like rabbits.

And while I'm discussing the Royal Family, just how much of the taxpayer's money did Prince Andrew pay-out in an out of court settlement to quieten his under-age penchant for young girl sex trysts? 12 million, was it? I bet old Fergie was pleased about that as she only got 3 million. A great use of our tax money don't you think?

Ask yourself, and be honest, what do we need to see in our Great British Empire as future leaders and visionaries that will take us forward, giving the nation a clear message of hope, unity, peace, positivity, and all with authentic transparency. People that you can look up to and admire because you want to be like them. How many do you count? Now I ask you to contemplate this for a few moments because I bloody love our country and not mentioning any names, there have been a few whom have thrown it to the dogs. No guessing who.

Let's take a walk down memory lane for a moment and investigate women's rights before the 1960's. Of which, the 'hatred' of men has been rippling out ever since. Margaret Thatcher famously said,' If you want something said, ask a man, if you want something done, ask a woman.'

Are these sentiments 100% true? Are they damaging to the masculine and feminine counterparts? Certainly, it did not appease the rift between the sexes, rather shooting the selves in the foot kitemark. Did this rise to men becoming passive aggressive as collectively they lost their purpose and respect? If we are going to base our reality on our experiences, did this attribute to girls becoming manipulative? We are not trained to be straightforward; we are hardwired to be good little girls. Later in life attracting a man who is either a child spouse, indicating a mummy wound or a man who will beat you into submission. The dangerous sort. See more in my Twin Flames chapter because you cannot turn a minivan into a sports car. Enjoy that unfolding for your own inner compass.

In the illusionary world of social media and muddy entanglement, everyone is an equal and a wanna be rock and roll star. Come on Liam Gallagher, you know it. As does the cheeky chappie Mr R Brand. AKA, sex on legs.

Stepping down off my wobbly soap box now. Feeling rather angrily agitated, can you tell?

Lastly, in truth, I didn't tell my Mum or Dad and the ones that I treasure, more often, that I loved them dearly. Every day I should have done this when I had the chance. For being the incredible humans that they were and for being brave to choose me. When you are struck with that urge, do tell another cherished other just how much you love them. For I know only too well, the sadness that I feel in not being able to do or show that in person now they are gone from this earthly plane.

To the biological beings who fostered my entrance into this world. Love to you too. I understand finally the sacrifices that, back in those days, you had no choice over. In our new emerging world, this disconnection is no more between humans.

My Mum, our Doris, used to say that 'blood isn't thicker than water.' Wise crone. Missed dearly. I love you.

Finally, my only wish in reading my chapter on Truth is that you find clarity in shaping, articulating, and feeling into your own. Did my words benefit, inspire, uplift, or resonate with you? Or did they make you feel reactive and charged? Either way, there is information there for you to navigate, contemplate and reflect on. My friends will often ring me up and invite me to some sort of social gathering, a fun event. Quite often I decline as I will be sitting on the sofa contemplating. Does this sound like your ideal date night of pleasure? For me, in this fast-paced way of instant gratification living, slowing down, and cultivating quiet is vital for me to process and self-enquire as to how I am responding or reacting in the world. This is from the old reactive version of me, the overweight and boozy version of Sarah. Or am I responding from a place of love, centred, and grounded in a space of wise neutrality?

These are my words.

Aho.

Darkness

Hello darkness my friend.

In this chapter, I'm going to take you on a little journey into the dark hole of my experiences. In my former lifetime, in the story that made up Sarah, she knew all about the dark shadows that lingered there because she lived them wholly. They followed her around like a black cloud, lingering and exploding whenever the downpour got the chance.

Let me tell you this, what you are about to read is not going to be a nice easy read, I do not want to project how it will make you feel but you might feel uncomfortable and triggered.

There is no light without darkness. This is true. For when you know darkness intimately, and fondly, you embrace the light, with grace.

I am not sharing this because I want you to feel sorry for me. On the contrary, I want you to be touched deep in your heart, to discover something new and alive within yourself, that you might not have ever come across before, so that you can know another's darkness, to relate it to your own inner world so that you find comfort in the unordinary, in that we are not alone in our madness. Nor was I mad. Perhaps, you will already have had similar experiences? These were very real indeed.

Are you ready??

Put the kettle on, get a nice relaxing cuppa in your comfy chair, and a few Kleenex tissues and then let's begin.

Let me enlighten you as to the content of my darkness list, to fore warn you of my conversations with you. It goes like this: Finding out that I was adopted, panic attacks, miscommunication with my parents, drinking, hiding my feelings from my ex-husband, seeing ghosts, distracting myself in my work and putting all my energy and focus into my kids. This chapter also contains information on me ignoring my overweight, boozy body and the seriousness of deaths that ensued and the hurt it brought about from the loss of my beloved brother, father, dog, Mum, and subsequent divorce. This chapter discusses a large proportion about my understandings into finding out about my biological parents, without telling any of my family. Fuck, heavy secret to keep, which gnawed away at my innards for a very long time. Skeletons in the cupboard syndrome?

I will start from the beginning and go along in order with the bits that I feel with add value and purpose to the unfolding story. To help you understand, maybe for yourself or someone dear to you that you know, to share in the sentiment that we are NEVER alone.

Let's begin, I am 10 years old, I'm not trying to hypnotise you but just taking you back on my magic carpet of imagery to recreate the scene. It's plum with navy blue swirls.

Settled? Ok.

These are my confessions.

So, it's early one Sunday morning, and I've been called into my Mum and Dads bedroom, the sun is shining brightly through their bedroom windows, highlighting their glowing faces, and freshly made mint green bedding. They are very happy. My Mum begins by telling me that I was chosen, but not born to her, and that I was in fact adopted. I remember my Dad just nodding with a wry smile on his face. I left the room. Dumbfounded. Parenthetically, this is the exact moment in time when I learnt to withdraw and shut down my feelings, somatically known as non-reaction mutism or dissociating. Either way, I learned to block out everything which manifested as aloofness during arguments from that point onwards, until I shone light upon this shadow as a grown adult.

Anyways, my memory then takes me to the bathroom in which I find myself standing in front of the bathroom mirror, hands outstretched and examining my fingers and their shape. I vividly remember asking myself, 'who am I?' I was 10 years old. Unknowingly, I began to self-enquire, and this was my first encounter.

A few months later, my family are packing up the contents of our family home in Liverpool, and I am unable to say my farewells to my friends in school as I am debilitated, choosing to lie on the couch for several weeks, frozen. We are moving to be closer my Mum's sister and her tribe, to a place where I perceive that people don't talk properly. They say buzz for bus, nowt for nothing, jaft fot for you must and many other weird and wonderful, odd expressions. Somehow, my father assumed that we wouldn't get a future job with a thick scouse accent. Yet, we would with a Lancashire one? Hmmm.

My Mum called for the doctor to see me, and he came with his hat and his bag and knocked on the door with a rat a tat tat. The doctor cannot find anything wrong with me. A dear girlfriend brought a cute yellow teddy for my leaving present. I held onto it tightly for months on end afterwards.

Some years later, I heard the word psychosomatic illness banded about. It seems, that my body had discovered how to drop into shutdown mode to protect itself when it did not know the language to communicate its needs. This behaviour lasted many years and beyond, into my adult life when faced with challenging upheavals. Remember when I told you what my ex-husband said to me in the kitchen? Well, that was my pattern, but I was unconscious of it, of any of my upsetting and challenging exchanges until recently, when I brought it into the conscious and gave it lashings of compassion and understanding to myself foremostly, and to others who experienced back lash of it at the time. I often meditate on this.

Living in our new home, I am grieving the loss of some very dear, scouse, childhood friends and I do not realise this. My Mum asks me what's wrong when she catches me staring into space or am reluctant to go play out on the back fields with some new Lancashire friends, which I'd freshly made in school. She lovingly projects that it's my adoption, which I'm thinking about, that's causing me all the sadness. Next thing you know, I have a new lemon track suit to wear or another latest outfit. I'm more than happy with that and enjoy strutting around the house showing off my new-fangled look.

Fast forward several years and I discover, to my complete surprise, that I'm pregnant, after a cider date night binge with the first serious man I genuinely loved and felt connected to on a deeper level. I swear down that I didn't categorically know how you got pregnant with the science and technicality behind it. For God's sake, I was still climbing trees and playing cricket with the boys until I was 16. Plus, my Dad was squeamish if any period or boys' stuff was ever mentioned. With 3 girls, what do you expect?

Besides, I was completely flat chested until 16 years and then, wham, those melons started to sprout, as did my first bleed. I was mortified and totally unprepared.

Still, I'm only 21 years and had been privy to the Blackburn Raves and acid house, trance dance scene. A baby? I'm still wet behind the ears myself. Plus, how could I bring shame on my family? My middle sister had already given birth at 19years old and now a second daughter pregnant as well? I anticipated an abortion. Our newest family edition was enjoying her doting grandparents, and I hated kids and told said cute baby to shut up once and drank her baby formula in my cup of tea when we ran out of milk.

I told you I used to be a right selfish cow.

My rave pals talked me into organising an abortion, 3 weeks later I booked it. However, one day while driving into Manchester, early one chilly morning, I'm sat, bumper to bumper in a traffic jam which is snail crawlingly slow, (no uncommon on the M6 at peak times) and I experience this butterfly sensation in my tummy as though this thing is talking to me and telling me that it is going to be born.

So, with my tail between my legs, I told my Mum and Dad before Coronation Street one evening and they were wonderfully supportive. My Mum warned me about the complications of abortions and right there and then, I knew that this baby was going to enter the world for a purpose. I didn't know anything else other than that, except that the baby's father welcomed the news too and that we both promised each to make a real go of it. His parents were both reasonable too. All was well. Relief. My mum put her tiny, wrinkly hand on mine, and I knew that I had secured my Mums blessing. There were no words exchanged but a deep feeling of knowing was sensed between our 2 hearts in that moment. I could do this. We could do this. I could bring this butterfly flutterby into the world through my body.

Of course, looming said abortion date, a friend of mine asked me if I was going to get it sucked out like a hoover. My raving days were over. So was our friendship.

This is where it gets interesting. Take a break if you wish, grab a cuppa, this next bit is complicated and thought provoking.

Here I am, we are, raising our beautiful son in our lovely little canal side cottage. I'm approaching 24 years old and then something grips my stomach in anguish. Out of the blue, I became preoccupied with my natural birth mother and father. Why did I become so curious to know about them, their history? As in the words of Richard Ashcroft, I found myself singing, 'is it the genes that made me, or my society or psychology?'

After tucking our beautiful blue-eyed boy into bed, I'd find myself sitting in the back room alone listening to Velvet Underground or MJ, totally random but listening to the darker tunes while sinking a few beers or smoking a few puffs on a joint. Even though this was something that I really didn't enjoy but, to what back then I thought would help me sleep and quieten my record player mind. Our son slept straight through, so I couldn't blame him for my lack of sleep. He could sleep on a washing line that kid. No, there was something much deeper lurking within my body mind.

After a few telephone conversations and a heart to heart with close family members. The dark, well-kept secret was revealed. The skeletons in the closet got a dusting down and all that…

Well here goes, it seems that I was destined for the Salvation Army as my birth mother was an under-age teen and my biological father was a heroin addict, both from Brixton in the swinging sixties. She was not allowed to keep me. Illegitimate pregnancy was a mortal sin back then. It turns out, I wasn't the only child placed under care, as my natural mothers' younger sister also gave birth to an illicit child. I believe that she was 14 years old and that she gave birth to a baby girl who was also adopted. The reason for this is that both parents were away in Hong Kong working for Lord James Montgomery, who ever that is, and left their 5 influential daughters in the care of their grandparents in roaring London. Can you imagine that. Hence, these beautiful girls were soon noticed by group of older cockney wide boys and the rest I'll leave to your fancy.

Hey presto, I am painfully conceived and named after the Dick Tracey super sad film.

Now then, here comes the twist. Said biological Mother has a conversation with older sister who knows of a Liverpool couple who desperately want a child, after trying for a baby of their own but with no joy. Adopted Mothers sister comes to view said baby and deems her ok, i.e., has all fingers and toes and no horns. Two weeks later said biological mother and adopted mother stand side by side on a grey, miserable wet day on a platform station in an affluent part of Hampshire to complete baby exchange. Privately of course.

On a double parallel, one is expressing deep tears of sadness while the other is expressing deep tears of joy. Note the simultaneous parallel. Life does that, balances out the transitions. Little me is in the middle, energetically soaking all this information up.

Funnily, to this day, and paradoxically, I feel this twin, dual emotion most days in life.

My paperwork is super sketchy from the social workers undetailed documents. However, a few years later and still in early infancy, I am officially adopted. In the meantime, my parents escape to Germany as my Dad has a new role in the Army to fulfil and, as my Mum quite honestly told me, several years earlier, that she didn't want any of 'my' natural family to steal me back until I was legally theirs.

Sounds harrowingly tragic, but it's true. My version that I perceived anyway.

Next, I find myself contacting biological mother via telephone and I feel mixed up. I then find myself in a brief conversation with my biological sperm donor, and I'm having panic attacks at the bottom of the stairs. We are enroute to sunny Blackpool for a family day out, and I ask my ex-husband to drive me home, despite the groans of rigor from our boy who is squirming around pushing against his child seat restraint. He was so looking forward to playing in the wavy water at Blackpool Pleasure Beach, while I couldn't help violently vomiting and shaking on the hard shoulder only 5 miles away. I really did try to go.

A few months later, my family birthday party ensues and after 2 glasses of wine I'm showing my new, purple bra and knickers set while running up and down on the tables. None of my family are amused and believe that I am on hard drugs. This was trauma trying to find a way out, I have since come to know. I literally lost hold of any self-control that I had that evening. Keeping such a big secret from the family that I loved, I felt as though I had betrayed them.

Several calming months later, I gather the courage to meet both biological individuals and guess what. I really want to feel something, but I don't. Instead, I feel a deep disloyalty to my parents and sisters and brother, and this fucks my head. I cannot reach out and talk to them about it, instead I bottle up even more. That's what feels safe to me. Then I have no more contact as it is just too difficult and painful. Then we lose touch. Pattern, pattern, pattern. See? Then all this gooey mess gets stored in the body until it cannot handle it anymore. Do you recognise the sorry sentiments of my words too?

Life goes on and then my ex-husband and I plan the arrival of our beautiful baby girl. This one was planned. Did I ever sit down and tell my ex-husband what was inside my head? No. I didn't know how to. Or where to start. You didn't complain back then, you just were grateful for having a roof over your head and 2 healthy, amazing kids. Nor did I recognise said pattern, pattern, pattern. Keep yourself safe Sarah, at all costs. Stay silent. Uphold the peace.

When did the overweight and boozy bit start? I can't honestly pinpoint it. What I do remember is this, I was working hard, planning, and preparing what I thought were creative lessons, enjoying a glass of wine each evening to help me mark 30+ 60+ books each night and stick in the relevant learning objectives for the next day, and them all being differentiated and marked in green or pink pen, depending on learning objectives met. I was exhausted, distracted and living off adrenaline. I also remember my Mum sitting on her own night after night with a bottle of her favourite German white wine. Paint stripper I called it. She was relaxing in her favourite comfy chair, while Dad was out at the pub. I cannot imagine how tough it was raising 4 kids, but she seemed to do it effortlessly, without complaining. Her device was a few glasses of wine at the end of a busy day. Did I download something here? My very own future coping mechanism for stress? For self-soothing? Using alcohol as a prop?

I walked my best buddy, Buster each evening across the serene farmland for my sanity, then poured a glass or 2, which became 3 then 4 of wine to level me out. Before, I knew it, I was stopping off at the newsagents for a can of full fat coke to give me a boost pre-work. I so needed a morning pep up. Did I ever deeply relax or get the nourishing sleep my body was craving? Looking back, the answer was a firm no. My nervous system was fried but I had become desensitised to it and had internalised that my jitters were normal. That any feeling of softness or relaxation were abnormal? That it was ok for my jaw to be tightly constricted, and for my shoulders to feel rock hard. What was my body storing for me? Dead fish?

After several years in this mode, it hit me hard. Death. Don't get me wrong, in-between there were many awesome and incredible family times together; camping, festivals, special marked occasions, family bake offs and party celebrations to remember. Our old house was the best for gatherings. But this chapter is in reverence to the darkness.

I will talk about my ghost experiences before I talk more on death.

So, I broke all contact with my biological side of life. I just couldn't cope with the influx of overwhelming emotions. Nor did I have anyone to share my innermost feelings with, but the labyrinth inside my spiralling mind. So, I began checking out spiritual churches. I have no idea why, but I did. As a result, I will share several of my most significant experiences. They really did happen, and my ex-husband always used to say to me, 'why do whacky things only ever happen to you?' Good question that isn't it. I never knew the answer. But oddly, they did only seem to happen to and around me.

One evening during a mystical seance, one of the spiritual leaders is trying to contact the dead asking for any messages, I left unamused. No-one had come through. I jumped in my trusty VW Golf, buckled my seat belt up and indicated to pull out when I felt this weird big, wet sloppy kiss on my forehead. Immediately, I burst into tears and drove home as fast as I could.

Scenario number 2. I'm washing the dishes and both my hands are immersed in the soapy suds, I'm miles away thinking about something or other, when I sense someone sneak up behind me, grab my waist and snuggle up intimately. Quickly, I spun around and shouted out, as I thought it was my ex-husband in jest. Fathom this? No-one was there.

A few weeks after this, I quit going to the spiritual church because one evening, we went out for dinner and locked the house up as you do. After a swanky lavish meal, we returned home a few hours later to find all the living room pictures were at a slant, the windows open, all the doors open and all the house lights on. Most weirdly was this, our dog, a Staffordshire Bull Terrier, who knew that he was not allowed upstairs or on our bed, had done both and was found cowering under our duvet which he had rolled into a nest and was hiding his face. Odd and freaky behaviour from him, a well renowned nanny guard dog.

On another occasion, while I was cooking dinner, I noted that the outside garden light would flicker on and off, on and off, even after an electrical check. There were no issues to be found. Interestingly, one of my sons' friends joined us for dinner one evening and suddenly the front room TV turned on and was blazingly loud. We just laughed and got up to turn the TV set off as we frowned. Until it turned itself on again! EEKKK.

These next few paragraphs will discuss the following little incidents that lead up to the shittiest of them all, which found me launching myself down the street bare foot, wild eyed, banging on the door of our local vicars in earnest. I was doing my upmost to cook a delicious family fry up at the time.

Let me share these next hairy experiences, I'll keep them brief and won't go into the drama too much. I wonder if you have ever had anything like this ever happen to you before.

Late at night, after several large glasses of vino, I'm lying-in bed when I'm abruptly woken up at 2:45am to what I believed was my son striding around the bed. He was the same height as him, 6 foot ish and wearing a black V-neck jumper, white t-shirt, and dark jeans, but he had long jet-black hair. I shouted out my son's name as he neared, I'm half asleep, but I vividly notice half his face missing as he brushed past my side of the bed before quickly disappearing through the bathroom en-suite door with his back sinking into it. I am numbed back into a comatose sleep.

On another shaky night, I woke up remembering feeling a ton weight lying on top of me, trying to penetrate me and this thing felt super heavy and sinister. I froze, I couldn't speak, shout out or move until it got what it wanted and left. My energy. Google told me that it was an incubus and a fucking big, creepy one at that, trying to penetrate me.

On another hairy occasion while jumping out the shower, I noticed that our full-size, free-standing mirror, which normally faced the bed, had been completely turned around to face the wall. After I had got dressed, I quickly took this item to the nearest charity shop as that freaked me out also. My ex-husband went bonkers as he was sick of me throwing things out without his consent. His regular routine after a hard day's graft was to check the wheelie bin. I've always been like this. We used to have a lovely retro red lips telephone handset. When my Mum rang on Boxing morning to inform us all about my brothers' suicide that evening, I unplugged the said phone, even though I loved it, and chucked it in the bin. Deep down, something inside of me knew all along about energy, and the different lurking types.

Anyhow, let me finish with this finale before I start waffling on about cleansing your aura and purification.

I'm stood over my Aga cooker, complete with retro pinny, diligently cooking bacon, eggs, mushrooms, tomatoes, hash brown, the full works. I'm humming away at Theme Time Radio by Bob

Dylan and the theme is weather. Funnily, its lashing down outside, or am I crying inside?

I've lined the plates up along the counter, ready to dish out generous portions (I'm a feeder) and our table is set. I go to open the fridge door, to add the cooked sausages and both packets have disappeared. I look everywhere, in every cupboard door, in every shopping bag. I had only just cooked them! And I vividly remembered putting them all in the fridge to cool down.

Then, the menacing garden light wouldn't stop going on and off, on and off. I jokingly started to 'talk to it.' No more words needed as I noticed how it responded. I was out the door quick as a flash and next thing you know, I'm sat in the lounge of our local vicars, soothing myself with a lovely cup of tea, while he is furiously writing all these crazy details down and listening carefully to every word. I'm relieved.

I left feeling reassurance and comfort in the fact that he arranged to visit our home imminently. I returned to a bowl of muesli for breakfast instead, settled in the knowledge that he had taken my telephone number and would be calling me soon.

What I am about to tell you next sounds darkly comical, insane, bizarre, surreal, unreal even, but it is 200 per cent true, and as authentic and as accurate an account as I can justify.

Grab another cuppa if you wish. All set? Let's crack on some more.

It is mid-week, around 5pm, it's a dark autumnal night. The vicar has arrived with an accomplice in tow. He carries and reads from his

Bible, while his accomplice follows him around the house flicking holy water around many places. In particular, I noticed that they seemed to focus the most attention on the internal corners of the house and door frames. I'm sat down on the sofa with our dog Buster, sandwiched between my legs, who proceeds to roll around and rub his back in the holy water that falls on the carpet at my feet when they pass by. Blessed Buster.

My ex-husband had been instructed to sit outside with our children in the campervan, much to the amusement of his business partner who had just dropped him off outside the house. He was gobsmacked, astonished even. His eyes followed these 2 characters through our bedroom windows in the dim of the black night sky. No, it wasn't Halloween, but it wasn't that far away.

The conclusion from our respected Christian pillars of community? A dark entity had attached itself to me from one of my visits to the spiritual church. It had entered our home and was hiding beneath the outside garden light switch in the corner of the kitchen. My ex-husband did not believe any of this. However, our vicar did go on to say that there is no light in the Bible without dark, that in essence dark entitles, and all aspects of life, co-exist. One cannot exist without the other. Fascinating material. I was enlightened immediately.

Subsequently, I began re-reading the Bible my Mum had gifted me, and highlighting in luminous marker pen, parts of the text which really stood out while placing dried, delicate coloured rose petals in cherished chapters in remembrance.

That's the end to that talk on my experiences regarding ghosts. After our vicars visit, we had no more incidents with missing sausages ever again.

Have you ever experienced esoteric things like these?

Now for my views on death, which is from my own perspective, please remain aware....

What is obvious from my own version of growing up is that my Dad, with his belt threatening days, and my Mum with her hair lacquer throwing episodes, are nothing compared to the nothingness that kids are currently suffering with today because of boredom. As a growing teen, I could at least fight against these measures. I distinctly remember telling myself that I wouldn't copy their behaviour when I became older. I was given a marker from which to stand my ground. I ate my tea, even if I did sneakily spit it in the bin afterwards, especially if it was corned beef hash or pea and ham soup. I really detested that gloop.

Unlike today's kids whose Mums are cooking 3 separate meals and the kids have absolutely everything, in possession form, that any child could possibly want. If these affluent kids have everything? Then why is there so much disconnection in the world? No wonder this aptly named snowflake generation find themselves identifying with a penguin if they so wish.

What I do know is this too. When I was a teenager, I began writing a lot of poems. I have no recollection of whom inspired me so. What I remember is feeling alone with my thoughts when my hormones kicked in and I got my first menstrual bleed. I was not a door slammer; I was a furious pen scribbler. Here's one of my very first scribblings:

Melodramatic feelings force my ink to write,
To release the tension from my mind,
And relax my system,
Such good therapy,
Stronger than any pills,
Just the cost of ink,
No large doctors' bills,
When times are low,
I need to be alone to write,
When times are lowered, I write a book,
Inspiration then comes naturally,
My brains overcharged,
My ink runs merrily,
I emerge refreshed and happy.

Wasn't I a moody, thoughtful bitch?

Seriously, on reflection I don't really think so. I feel that my emotional intelligence was not supported or even recognised wholly. No fault or projection here on anyone. I'm taking ownership of this. It has taken me 40+ years to understand who I am on every level (and I'm still finding out more!) My work is not done, nor will it ever stop, until my toes are stiff and I'm enjoying corpse pose for good.

In my day, the focus was all on cognitive intelligence. Allow the developing, spongy brain of a child to cram learn so many facts, call it cross curricular learning to aid long memory recall. But don't and I mean don't discuss the mind, behaviour, or feelings or open that can of worms. Keep spirituality in the context of the church and its doctrinarian. Let the girls flash their panties while doing handstands against the wall. Allow the boys to play 'catch and grab the girl' and roughly fondle the scared chosen one, pawing over her clothes to gain unlawful access to her growing female, tender form. I have said this before but Aldous Huxley, a well renowned philosopher who stated over a century ago that education needed to balance a masculine heavy curriculum and balance it out with emotional, more feminine intelligence. Excuse the pun. Yet, why is emotional intelligence deemed more female? Is it because us women are more feelers due to our hormones and owning the womb of man? Able to seed the manifestation of God's glory? Babies! Possibly, one of the reasons why women statistically have more mental health problems and men commit suicide. Just a thought.

My Dad was the greatest man in the world. Why wouldn't he be? I doted on him. From being as small as I can recall, he was the apple of my eye. Not my Mum, she was the bad cop, the one who made all the decisions and did everything. My Dad was the good cop, he luckily received that playful role. He worked hard and came home to a hot meal every night served on the table. I hardly remember him cooking, slaving away in the kitchen, peeling spuds with a knife, reading the newspaper with a fag in his gob, or stuffing an endless stream of dirty laundry in the washing machine. Nope. He did make a mean fried rice and chicken curry with apple and raisins in when he got the chance. They felt like special occasions. After a hard day's graft, all the little kids in our street would run out to dangle off his legs and pull on his key chain, eager to get a glimpse of his wicked smile and jovial quick step as he strode from his parked car. We were rich because we eventually owned a car! Wasn't I the lucky one who got to twirl on his fingers and stand on his polished boots for a boogie while the rest of the street kids looked on in glee and so wanted a turn? I was beyond thrilled!! This was my Dad and he belonged to me. Little did they know that once behind the closed door, he plonked himself Infront of the TV while us kids got to cuddle on his knee if we were quiet enough. Desperate to hear one of his stories, we'd wait patiently and would sit staring at the TV, usually Coronation Street, until a question arose. Like the time I asked what 'gay' meant after the notorious no chin Gail Tilsley (she made my Dad grumble) flipped some remark. I was told to wait until I was 16 to be told what this meant. I was about 8/9 years at the time, but this has always stuck with me. Like the time my younger, middle sister choked on bacon fat while sitting on my Dad's knee. He shot up and whacked her back so hard, I remember feeling as shocked to see him hit her that I thought that I was going to die instead.

    I'm not going to lie; I had a super strong connection to my Dad. For the first 5 years of my tiny life, I had him all to myself and I relished in that. I'd get sick when he went away in the army for a long spell. My Mum noted how withdrawn my behaviour became in his absence. I was attached and loved him dearly. That was until the rest of the brood came along and I was no longer the star of the show. That's when things started to change, and I started playing up. I became the clown to get any sort of attention. I'd daydream and start creating other worlds in my head. Looking back, how tiring must having 4 kids under 5 be? So, I decided I was having the boy twin to compensate. My middle younger sister would have the girl, Pongo Lil because her nappies stunk the most. I had the prized, Ginger Nut, and I treated him like a king. My attention had changed focus on this super adorable, dimply little bundle of laughter. My Dad could go to the pub every night after work for a few pints. My warrior Mum organised the 4 kids and housekeeping. She was the captain of the ship and indestructible. The more we grew, the more he seemed to shut down and supress any emotion with alcohol. To this day I have no idea what was going through his head. He did have a very stressful job and shared a few dark horrors of his experiences on CAT C Ward, the big jail house. Like the time an inmate had barricaded the door of his prison cell with a mattress. All the alarms were going off, but by the time they got to him, all that was left was his singed hands clinging to the iron bars. Another time, we were on holiday in sunny Wales when my Dad started to usher us out of the shop and down some trashy side alley, huddling us together until someone has checked past us. My Dad often got weird cards in the post. Once, I found a stick man drawing with his hanging face sketched on. It was a hand-made card, but it was obvious that someone disliked him. I have no idea why? Nor did my Mum ever say anything about this, although I knew that she was often scared, and chain-smoked a lot more when particularly experiencing emotional overwhelm.

My Dad grew up in a time when men didn't go to the doctors to seek help. Come on, he was a war veteran. He had a bamboo tattoo when stationed in Borneo. He had too much pride! What if the neighbours found out? Nor did he talk about his feelings, instead he bottled them up, he manned up. What is man about this? Men in the 70's and 80's worked their balls off every day in a job they probably didn't like but it paid them wages and gave their families a roof over their head and food on the table. And you ate what you were given, or you went hungry. Men were the bread winners, the providers, the patriarchal epitome of a solid family society. Looked up to, listened to and respected in those days. Plus, you certainly did what you were told and never complained, because back then, kids feared their Dads whether they hit them or not. You didn't mess with your Dad. My Dad is bigger that your Dad and all that. And if you didn't have a Dad in school, you were bullied.

My Dad really started to soften when his new grandkids arrived. His daily drinking was now the norm and accepted. He never was loud and leary, more silent and deadly. He fell in love with his first granddaughter, I remembered that doting feeling. He became alive again and this was so awesome, well for a wee while. This is where my brother comes in. However, I do need to add a bit more so that the whole picture is formed, from my perspective, you see, my Dad's Dad evolved into an alcoholic. He lived and breathed and was a landlord of a famous boozer in Everton, Liverpool. When I was a small girl, I remember singing the 'wheels on the bus,' while skipping along the bar, much to my amusement and entertaining showbiz self. Oh, more attention, I lapped it up even from the greying old eyes of the drunken, stumered, wrinkly men. I do recall the carpets stinking of smoke and a strange wee smell though. Despite this, I would still eagerly go to sing for my Dad in the pub. I loved him with all my heart, and still do, because the heart does not have an on/off switch, it just loves. Nor does it know when the physical body has gone, our heart chamber, has a little energy bubble which always resonates on the love frequency. Now isn't that magic?

Brother...

The hole...
The door to the hole is shut tight,
Hiding the bare walls, floors,
Smell of shite,
Oh, brother dear brother,
What is the answer,
What is the question?
No-one can touch you,

You're in the hole.
Don't you want to get out and make something of it?
Or close the door,
Close the world,
Close your dreams and goals,
Climb into a bed full of cig burns?
Search for that hero inside of yourself,
Grab the bull by the horns,
Make it happen,
Some might say,
There won't be that day,
Grit your teeth,
Don't be daft,
Make yourself proud,
Make you laugh,
Close the door to the hole and never look back,
Never look back,
Brother dear brother,
The hole is very dark,
You can't see what you are in,
Others can,
Let some light in,
Let some light in.
Brother, dear brother,
I love you.

After Mum and I found that sticky, brown stained spoon under his bed, the unravelling of his darkness and manifesting addictions began. It wasn't long before we noticed money going missing, and the ensuing, blatant lies. When you truly know the internal experience that someone is going through, whom you deeply love, and who simply cannot help telling lies to get what they crave, that is a different kettle of fish. Somehow you learn to forgive quickly and let it go. On the other hand, if someone is telling lies for the sake of control and manipulation purposes to win something over in you deliberately, consciously doing it, there is a real difference. Be careful with that one. Those types of lies are the narcissistic ones. My little brother was showing this challenging behaviour unconsciously. It was driven by a deep desire to get his needs met, to numb his inner pain. He really struggled as a kid, and I'll explain why shortly. He was not a narc. He was experiencing continual, internal, emotional turmoil. For those of you who have experienced the turmoil the hook brings, you will know that having a heroin addict in the family brings immense suffering and complete frustration at the inability to really help them come back from their stupor. I didn't care if he stole my camera or golf clubs or the cash, which I dropped off at his house to pay my Mums loan that went missing. She went ballistic at me on the phone for that one, so I ended up writing out a cheque book wadge, post-dated with £50 amounts to settle my debt with her. A cheque book indeed, remember that? Unbeknown to her, my little bro had stuck it in his toe veins as he'd ran out of arm parts. Thankfully, he didn't lose his legs, or have any body parts amputated like a former friend of his, nor did he immediately die of an overdose, but his passing came in another torturous way that affected my Mum the most. He just couldn't hold onto the sensitivities of life anymore. After that, my Dad just shut down on all levels and that is when his manifested sickness began inside his own emotional body, which eventually concluded with his own traumatic passing.

Why choose the pathway of heroin? Now that is a great question. I've contemplated this for many years, and I still don't know the answer. Was it because the school thought he needed specialist help on his learning journey? Did he have undiagnosed ADHD? He couldn't sit still, he found reading, Maths and English assignments difficult. He would run out of his classroom at the speed of lightening if confronted with a task. Standing up to answer a question freaked him out. How did I know? Our primary school was open plan. I witnessed his beautiful head of ginger hair flying across the milk carton counters, most often knocking them all over, resulting in more teacher moans at sticky, milky, goo on the floor! I found this totally hilarious behaviour. Pre-school, I babied him. I dressed, fed, read to him, sat him on my knee and put bunches in his hair and once dressed him in a nighty because he felt left out as the only boy. OMG, I really loved doting on him. He was my little, real-life, boy doll. Once, as an adorable baby, I took him out in my broken, wobbly 3-wheel pram. Unharnessed, I carefully placed him, probably at around 3 months old, in my battered, orange Silver Cross Pram, and gingerly wheeled him down our 3 huge concrete steps right outside our front door, tottering off to God knows where, when my Mum came screaming and soaring out of the door faster than Hussein Bolt. I vividly remember her white aghast drop-dead jaw, and her curly bob almost standing on an electrical edge! I was unfazed, I sincerely thought I was just going to take him for a nice walk somewhere along the railway lines. How innocent children were back in the good old days. Now I thought she was seriously over-reacting.

Jesus, I remember another time my brother and his twin sister Pongo Lil, (stinky nappies) decided, in their little matching cherry red and sky-blue snow suits, to unleash the back garden gate and undertake a sneaky micro adventure along the back-alley ways and onto the main road. Shit a brick, my Dad was out at work and my Mum dragged us around the estate looking for them. We did eventually find them stopping the traffic as our Pongo had taken her Fisher Price pull along pooch with her, and a passing car had run over the long lead and had snapped it. Our Pongo was standing at the side of the road observing a splatted, wooden doggy in bits, standing heartbroken with a dangly bit of string in her hands while wearing an upside-down smile with teardrops sprinkled on her blush cheeks. My brother was just standing right next to her side, on the pavement (thank God) looking on. Thankfully, no child was killed, only the toy doggy, and that was tragic enough. The terrible twins were always getting up to mischief. They were so funny and really did bounce of each other.

Something to reflect on is this. ADHD and ADD and other such illness were quite unheard of back then. Not many professionals seemed to note the adverse reactions from the mercury and aluminium vaccinations given to new-born babies. Even the Vitamin C jab was soaked in the toxic stuff? With an increase in this physiological challenging way of living, just a thought but has the ingredients changed? Increased in toxic quantity? Who regulates this? Who safeguards our future generations and are they necessary these days in a society whereby the diseases of the past no longer threaten our health, as healthcare and the quality of our life is far superior in the Western world than the days of yesteryear? For example, do we need to invest our money on the 6 in 1 vaccine when collectively, we could be spending our money on far greater and more worthy causes? Does metal toxicity affect girls and boys cognitive functioning, and hormonal levels differently? Is that why more boys are diagnosed with this disorder as it affects those with testosterone more so? Just a thought.

My brother also loved to play the adventurer. On rainy days he would get us to pack Dairylea cheese sandwiches in a rucksack, a colouring book, a lightweight jacket, pretend tools, always a hammer, and off we go, up a mountain, climbing on the 3 flights of angled stairs. Resting for our picnic at the basecamp. We'd grab each other's ankles, and crawl down on our bellies, or we'd take the mattress off the bed and carefully roll up the front to slide down the avalanche. Oh, we had the best fun on those long wintery nights, climbing mountains and using our little imagination to the max. The game that my brother loved the most, probably because it was rough and involved fast moment and plenty of shoving, was the 'Wizard of Oz,' Game. Us kids would stand in the four corners of the room and spin about to this song, then meet in the middle like a kind of hootenanny to link each other's arms and spin even faster!! That is, until my brother stuck his foot out, tripped someone up, then roughly dove on them to release the tickle monster both purposefully and gleefully. Albeit it was a bit rough in my remembering. Our visiting cousins loved this fast paced, physical, childish game too. It tired us all out in heaps of giggles in a big puppy pile on the living room, psychedelic orange, brown and green swirly carpeting.

Growing up, we had many fun times. I learnt to get to know that boys were very different, irrespective of having a tail. We were so blessed to use our imagination which our Mum and Dad encouraged. They encouraged us to play shop with mud, build bike ramps with scraps of old furniture, play pretend hairdressers with REAL scissors in the garage, I won't go further with that one. My brother and I liked to make dams in the river and build little campfires. Until a friend's parent spotted us in the back fields, smoking rolled up leaves with my Dad's pinched tobacco spied through his binoculars. My brother loved to take the nib out of felt tip pens then draw all over his hands, or a dolls face. After he had cut the hair off it. Experimentation was encouraged from an early, curious age.

The best story I'll save in my sister's section. Hold on for that one. It involves a broken arm. God knows how my Mum and Dad kept sane!! They certainly allowed us to be creative.

Then what happened to him to lead him to drug taking?

To be honest I'm not sure. Was it the community of like-minded, other bored boys, living in a low social status, working class town? Did they feel that they were good enough? Hhhmmm. Let me see. This might resonate with you too.

Once my Mum told me to get my brother for tea. We didn't have mobile phones back then. We went home when the streetlights went off. I skulled around the streets of our estate until I found him in his friend's garage with a plastic bag in his hand, eyes rolling, one is Chester, the other is in Manchester, his lips were inflamed, cracked and spotty. I noted several arenol cans on the floor. As a growing teenager I was naive, was it glue or another high substance? I'm not sure, but I dragged him home anyway and sobered him up on the way back, before we had our corned beef mash and beans for dinner. Ask Google did not exist back then.

I feel that that was the start of his journey experimenting with glue, aerosols, weed, cider, vodka, coke, heroin, snowballing right up until his mid 30's. It stuck with him. He seemed to enjoy the chilling buzz out of it.

In his favour, he did live with a partner and have 2 beautiful boys whom I still love to see. Sadly, for 2 years we all knew that he would one day take his life. Just like Judas, 3 times he tried it, it was inevitable. As a family we didn't know what to do, how to communicate our internal experiences around this, how to help, could we even help, was it too far? He'd woken me up at 2am in the morning, crying at the top of a multistorey car park, telling me that he was about to jump off. I jumped out of bed in my P'J's and frantically searched several known locations. I drove home depleted, just hoping that he hadn't done it. He didn't that time but was found with 2 slashed wrists at the bottom of the lane near A&E.

After a short spell in a mental hospital over Christmas, I knew he felt safe, our carrot top did. He had structure and a routine and was given regular medication. He played pool and spoke about running a marathon, which meant that he was feeling positive and planning to turn his life around.

Sadly, despite his best intentions and kindly shovelling the snow off his neighbour's drive to release some much-needed built-up energy, he just couldn't cut the mustard. After a while, you learn the difference between holding a hand and chaining a stoic soul. Also, his drug choice changed form as he opted for the Ray-Ban smoke and mirrors ego kind. Trendy at the time. It was around this time that I decided to opt out of what Stephen Karpman first destined in 1961 as the triangle of drama, referred to as the victim, rescuer, and persecutor syndrome. I was tired and sick and tired of feeling sick and tired, and I couldn't work a way out to fix anything. So, I surrendered and let go of everything and turned my attention on my kids and their happiness. Notice how I didn't say my happiness?

Boxing day 2009, the house phone rang, a red pair of lips plugged into the wall by a chord. Hello? It's my Mum. 'He's done it,' was all she said. Numb, I unplugged the phone from the connection socket and put it in the wheelie bin, as I mentioned before. Such a shame as I really did love that retro collector's item. Though, I was in deep shock, I couldn't cry. I couldn't go to see him. He'd used the sleeve from his favourite Everton top to wrap around his neck on a low protruding silver birch tree not 10 metres from his house. His partner screamed from her front doorstep. An early morning passer-by on route to her care home employment found him frozen, still, and motionless. God bless that girl as that image of him will stay with her forever. Thankfully, the Malcolm in the middle went to identify his body, the sister with the beautiful face and heart to match.

Time is a healer they say. The body mind never forgets. That was one of the saddest days of my life. Anyone who has experienced this will know the tragedy that rips through a family after such a devastating loss.

Another crueller one, was seeing the demise of our Mum. For 4 years she became a recluse, fearful of going out and of her own mind. A noise from the roof, or simply putting the bins out, would send her into turmoil and her nervous system into dysregulation. A meditation CD was her only friend and thank God she listened to that on loop. Sadly, her hair grew long and pale and the light extinguished from her eyes. It was so heart-breaking to stand and communicate through the window, as during that period I wasn't allowed in. She had stopped hiding her beer in a mug, it was on view, on the coffee table. All care gone.

This one time, I received a distressed phone call from her, she knew that it took 20mins to arrive by car from my work. I went and did and found her naked, white eyes rolling, foaming at the mouth and rolling on the floor ready to pass out. I noted an empty box of sleeping tablets in the wastepaper basket, alongside heavy anti-psychotic meds. I dialled for a blue light immediately as my Dad calmly rolled another fag and turned the tv channel over.

When the paramedics arrived, they asked me several questions. I remember saying that her heart is broken, and she is suffering from that intense emotion. She never got over the traumatic death of her only son. Her saddening ramblings in her journal confirmed this.

Rest in peace my baby brother.

I will always love you and miss your daft sense of humour so much. This is the workings of an uncleared monkey mind, and heart. This was my wisdom from the darkness that followed for several years as I tried my best to comprehend the precious loss of much-loved human beings. This naturally led me on my quest to help myself, and others struggling internally. This was my biggest gift to learn how to compassionately turn a crisis into a blessing, without spiritually by-passing a thing.

Further dark confessions: I have a middle sister, the middle one, whom I used to call Miss Piggy as a horrible hormonal teenager. She used to be a chubby girl and once, scoffed a whole packet of Penguin biscuits before our Mum and Dad had had the chance to put the supermarket shopping away. She has such a beautiful face and heart to match in all ways though. She is a warrior hearted sister who never ceases loving. I remember one time, noticing empty colourful foil packets blowing down our tarmacked driveway. I also noticed her bedroom window open. Miss Piggy would also wipe her snot under the sofa armrest in a big swoping line when engrossed in the TV. She really did love picking her nose. The youngest, and the twin to our brother often titled 'the twinnies,' was fondly called metal mickey for her braces or Pongo Lil, depending on my mood. Once I ripped off the jeans, she'd stolen out of my bedroom wardrobe, literally off her legs as she swanked past in the lounge. Thought she could go out swanking in my best Levi jeans, did she? Also, when she was 8 years old, mischievously, I decided to tie our bikes together with some old rope that I found in the garage. Then, with me on my trusty, red chopper and her on her tiny, gold budgie bike, we wheeled to the top of a nearby, long driveway. One, two, three, weeeeee!! We were enjoying freewheeling together down the hill, this was a great experiment. Until her tiny budgie bike flashed past me with a golden shimmy. Next thing you know, Pongo Lil has overtaken me, she's now dragging my bike at top speed. Then, my brakes lose their power and the rope snaps. Crash, bang, wallop, our Pongo is lying on top of a twisted, funny looking arm. I've never seen anything like that before. It did look weird. I ran home as fast as I could screaming. Turns out our Pongo had broken her arm in 2 places. Mum went berserk.

Talking of budgies, we used to have a luminous green and yellow pet one named Joey, until one sunny afternoon my friend found it asleep in the bottom of its cage. It slept for 2 whole weeks until it disappeared, cage and all one day. We had also had several funfair goldfish pets, until they resembled lifeless carrots lying at the bottom of a murky, goldfish bowl.

The middle one was such a good girl and peace maker. She would never inflict any harm like that. Although she did run away from home once with her panda teddy, all the way down the tarmacked driveway to sulk outside the front door. And she used to drive us mad by singing the Annie song before bedtime every night. Our Pongo used to like kissing the older boys in our garage too. I think she would have made a great sex therapist.

I love my siblings for very different reasons. It sure was like the tale of Little Women in our house. Crazy but I loved that, and both of my sisters to the moon and back. However, in my darker years, I'm sincerely sorry for being a pain and telling lies to Mum when it was me who wrote that naughty condom poem. I forgot who I blamed but I purposefully changed my handwriting style deliberately, so that no-one would find out that it was me.

I am a big-time dog lover. I feel that the great mystery gives us these companions in life so that we learn unconditional love, for there is no other animal that will love you more than it itself. One of the saddest days of my life was when my Buster died at 11 years old. He still had so much umph left in him. Further confession time.

So, we've already given a dog away since it almost put my ex-husband in hospital following an asthma attack. It was that severe that he couldn't walk down the stairs even though we had a bungalow at the time. The dander in the skin of those walking rug variety apparently triggers allergies. After a heartbreaking decision this fluff pot goes to another home. Our children are mortified. Two weeks later, ex-hubby is recovering well, and I am on the dial up internet watching the blue line travel across my screen. The doctor told me about Staffordshire Bull Terriers being good for allergies or Mexican Hairless dogs. So, I am scrawling, looking for a nanny dog to rescue while waiting for a blue line to unfold. Dogs are for life not just for Christmas.

The Christmas walk is going well, the ex-hubby and I are enjoying a walk over the golf course. The pooch has run off to scoff something he has sniffed out in the distance across the fields. He is busy, greedily scoffing something hidden under the bushes. By the time I sprinted to get there whatever it was had been demolished. I'm angry at him and shout out loud, then put him on his lead for a while. Staffordshire Bull Terriers do have a habit of running off, especially if there are ducks or squirrels about, it drives them nuts. If you have had one, you'll know what I mean. Naughty Buster.

Anyway, 10 mins later his back legs jut backwards, his dark brown eyes start rolling and he's frothing at the mouth. In amazement, next thing is he's dropped to the floor, and I can feel his body is stiffening up. We take turns carrying him home. He really isn't well.

Arriving home 20 minutes later, our Buster is wanting to go outside to cower in the corner of our garden, in his favourite spot, quietly and bravely with this intense bodily sickness that is taking over his life slowly by shutting down his organs. Next, we have an urgent telephone call with the local vet who reckons that he has been poisoned, his initial diagnosis from his behaviours suggested that he had ingested a rather large amount of anti-freeze. It is too late. I'm fucking heart broken, and we are all sobbing our eyes out. The neighbour next door must have suspected blue murder.

He's wrapped in his Dad's favourite woollen, red checked hiker jacket that we jokingly referred to as the 'rapists' jacket,' No explanation needed. It was a household joke. My daughter and I keep a teary vigil throughout the night. Dog lover friends, you will know if you know that I have no more words to tell you, the angst felt.

Dear Buster, the holy water did not save you this time.

The local paper was informed, and a small piece was written about farmers and their practise of using and applying anti-freeze and a food combo mix to keep foxes away from their livestock, in our case it was chicken carcasses and carrots, Christmas leftovers, which is a common and widely practised deterrent apparently.

So, all these traumatic life events are muddled up and stored in my guilty, regretful body mind. They are so varied, and I don't know what to do with all this material. We are not taught self-regulation in schools from an early age like they are in the East. What happens to my tiny frame? It expands with the toxic thoughts, foods, drinks, and chemicals that I am both drinking, bathing in and thinking constantly. I am holding all this stuff with no real outlet, just dumping more and more toxic stuff in there. Before you know it, I'm a balloon. What happens when you are chockfull?

Jesus Christ, please forgive me, I am a sinner and nothing but a filthy rag.

No words.

Light

Light. The Bibles description:

Light was the first thing created and among the first words spoken by God that were written in Scripture: "Let there be light!" (Gen 1:3). As the first created thing and something necessary for life, light holds primary significance in the Bible. Throughout Scripture, light imagery is consistently used to symbolise life itself, particularly life lived in a way that pleases God.

Just a thought, if you believe that God "spoke" the first command about creating the world, then couldn't it be argued that a sound initially created or commanded the universe into existence because words are made from sound.

In a world where the dark night was fraught with danger, light was a fitting image for safety. For example, Light from God is similarly featured in the deliverance of the Israelites from Egypt: "But because of your endless compassion, you didn't abandon them in the desert.

More so, the light of Christ present in the people's hearts is a symbol for salvation. Those who follow him do not walk in darkness, but in light (John 12:46).

Light also reveals what is hidden. That's why we say things "come to light" when they are discovered. However, it can have multiple meanings, the same as we use light today. It can be the light of the sun or the flame of a lamp. It can describe the weight of an object. It can mean the weight of a burden or problem. It is interesting that in Genesis

1:3, God declares "Let there be light". But then in Genesis 1:14-19, God that establishes the stars, sun, moon, sets it all in motion. Clearly 2 different sources of light which God describes himself literally as 'it.' But the most common use describes the revelation of God. John 12:35, Jesus said to them, "The light is among you for a little while longer. Walk while you have the light, lest darkness overtake you. The one who walks in the darkness does not know where he is going.

Is the darkness your companion?

Without the experience and intimacy of knowing the darkness, there is no understanding of the joys of living in the light of the Almighty, I will refer to as God (and you know why). This is when you come to know the joys of liberation and connection and of trusting in the process. This is the time when you accept, and surrender your whole being up in absolute trust. A period of acceptance, permission, of opening the heart, yoni, and soul, of taking time to make love. To allow the masculine to penetrate you. To be consoled as to console and be loved as to love and understand as in the words of ST Francis of Assis. Don't you just love those sentiments? There is light but it is a choosing a limitless freedom in the knowing that every day there are miracles to be had. The feminine way is of softness. Dare to be vulnerable, dare to be empowered, dare to be authentically you on every single part. Can you do that in isolation? No. Another human, with a matched resonance is required to supply that evolution. That is the definition of grace in working motion at its finest in this great tapestry we call life.

Have you suffered in the darkness and bathed in the light too? Can you recognise it but not get too attached to it? Or are you at the stage of seeking the sensual pleasures and gratification of the light through externals such as plant form, i.e., magic mushrooms? Even over gym exertion can be ego identification and give a false sense of bathing in the light. More akin to the grasping of a moment in time, of an altered state of escapism that could be identified as 'more connected to source?' A hormonal hit of ecstasy. A portal change in the brain? Forced expansion or relaxed intention?

I fondly remember my first and only meeting with the great Mother of all plant medicine…Ayahuasca. I only needed to sit with her once as I received all I ever needed in that one session. Here's how it went after the necessary preparations to cleanse the body and mind to a more natural state of balance, less the toxic sugar, wheat and dairy which had crept into my diet and expanded my muffin top somewhat.

So, the intimate group of like-minded others are collectively sat in the temple with buckets at the ready. We are all dressed in white clothing, while sat in a pyramid format facing one another. The medicine is handed out by the shamans and loving prayers are shared.

Then the wait begins.

Time and space have stopped still. However, as I look up at the skylight, I'm aware that it must be around 7pm. I notice the dusky light shing through the glass above.

The next thing you know is that I'm staring at a ferocious looking wolf in my mind's eye, I am not aware of the sex of this magnificent creature, but I am staring right back into one luminous green eye and one azure blue. Its fur is mixed shabby, grey, and blackish white speckled. Once it knows I am not frightened nor perceive it is a threat, it slopes off to the side to reveal a tunnel of light and what looks like a male silhouette leaning against the curved entrance. I am welcomed further, beckoned even, to go further towards this mystical doorway. I am not aware of any physical body that I have, only a sense of seeing visually. Nor is there any sound, or smells, just a feeling of floating but not in my body if that makes sense. What I remember next is rather amusing. I found the formless body floating in a black void for the next 7-8 hours. It was sublime. Think of the dark night sky, look up, visualise that and I was that black, cosmic universe, just suspended like the sensation you get from being in a floatation tank, only I was experiencing being everything and nothing at the same time. Calm.

I realise that I can hear music, it is so beautiful, detailed, journeying like an orchestra of layered intrinsic pieces. I open my heavy eyelids. The shamans are grey, aliens, slim, slender fingered ET's who are playing this exquisite music from their stomach area, this divine sound is coming from that specific region. They have these huge black, slit eyes, sitting on the side of their oval head.

I look around the room, the guy opposite me is moaning intensely from the depths of his soul and rolling from side to side on his temple cushion. Another guy in the opposite corner has sprouted 2 additional bodies, like lord shiva and each one in turn is acting out a different psyche part. The guy to my right has a barbed wire mesh, wrapped around his head with buzzy bees attacking his facial parts in consecutive attempts.

I look at my hands and they are a kaleidoscope of colours, then I notice that they meet and merge with everything else in the room in Aztec bright pattern formations, pumping with electrifying force. I note that everything is poignant, so intricate, and fascinating to observe that a knowing arises in light information. Mind-bending.

What's more, I have enjoyed many tender moments with the Cubenzos mushroom variety. They did open a portal in my mind and directly made me feel at one with nature, as nature itself, but that was a small-time frame during the winter months to pep up a low mood. The sun is so healing, and we don't get enough of it in the UK. I tried their medicinal properties for my own learning as my vitamin D daily dose coupled with icy cold dips wanted a booster.

I am my own guru.

Do we really have trust in our back stories? Are they really who we are? Or are they teachings to bring us into wholeness at a later stage in life?

This I feel is true.

Light is information on all levels. But it is in kindness and compassion to the self on the deepest level and of the opening of the body mind to that. I mean it is felt with awareness in each simple moment. It is the noticing. It is getting out of your own way. It is the golden, glittering moments of rich knowledge that seeps into a cherished moment in time. It could be an internal fuzzy feeling that you get from patting your pet. Or it could be the external delights of a pink blazing sunset, reaching far out across the skies. Then you are honouring your light and welcoming the joy and aliveness that each moment can bring.

I vividly remember visiting my Mum, during one of her several mental health sectioning's, to find myself smothered in the middle of a puppy pile of patients. Like moths attracted to the light of mine, I knew they could feel it, I'm going to let it shine. After several moments of giggling and hugging, the nurses peeled them off me 1 by 1 and ordered them back into their day room for quiet. My Mum was launching felt tip pens around as darts and all 5 feet of her was dragged off to a private side room, and I witnessed her being pushed down on the bed and given a swift injection in her bare backside. A while later, upon resume of my visit, she started talking in riddles and believed that I had flown in from India in a hot air balloon and had fortunately landed in the middle of the hospital courtyard. And, she found it bloody hilarious when I took a sip out of her water bottle after her telling me, with a cheeky glint in her eye that she had mouth thrush. Her own Mum, our pixie Nana, had received electric shock therapy to ease her mental symptoms. We wouldn't let ours. The medication was bad enough.

Consider this statistic for a minute, in 2012 the US public spent $1,526,228,000 on Abilify, more than any other antipsychotic in the US. The new generation of antipsychotics such as Abilify, Risperdal, Zyprexa or Sequel are top selling drugs in the US. Number three? Cymbalta, an anti-depressant that sold over a billion dollars' worth of pills, even though it has never been shown to be superior to Prozac.

Let that sink in for a moment.

What's more, Medicaid, the government health aid for the poor, spends more on antipsychotics than any other class of drugs. In 2008, it funded $3.6 billion for antipsychotic medication. Shockingly, half a million children currently take antipsychotic medication in the US, for young people under the age of twenty that number is constantly increasing.

Meanwhile in the UK, I Googled annual data from NHS Digital that showed in 2016 NHS Prescriptions in England was 64.7m for antidepressant items. That was 3.7m more than the 61m items dispensed during 2015.
It also represents a massive 108.5% increase on the 31m antidepressants that pharmacies dispensed in 2006.

Of course, they seem to make people more manageable and less aggressive, but they also interfere with motivation and creativity which are fundamental for well-balanced, contributing members of society.

Furthermore, try to find any research on alternative, more holistic approaches and that is like finding hens teeth.

Over the years, antipsychotics have become a norm in our culture but if they are so beneficial and effective as we are led to believe, why is depression not a minor issue in our society?

Yes, I get that anti-depressants can make the difference between day-to-day functioning. If it comes to a choice of taking a sleeping pill or drinking yourself into a stupor at night to get a few hours of sleep to numb out the pain, I know which I'd prefer, having tried both. Yet for those trying to sweat it out in a yoga class, without guidance, or trying out any other workout routine, solo motivation can be tough. As is the minefield of self-care and loving daily rituals and practices to work uniquely for everyone. You certainly can't paint people with the same brush!

What is evident is that mainstream medicine is committed to healing through chemistry, the fact that we can change our own physiology and inner sanctum by means other than drugs, is barely considered.

In the West we are defined by chemistry and talking therapy, yet in the East, Meditation, movement, rhythm, and action are used as a helping tool for trauma stored in the body.

For example, Yoga in India, African drumming, or Tai Chi in China, which leads me to share my own experience. Several years ago, I could not articulate why, but I felt unbearable sensations in my body. After actively trying numerous, failed, Western approaches, I took ownership of my healing and embarked on my journey around the world to reclaim my body mind and spirit. At the time, I felt completely lost and numb and without the right signposts or helping tools under my belt. I felt that I had no choice. I knew that I could not avoid these feelings deep inside of me that were making me feel so overwhelmed. This is how I came to know and understand body awareness, which puts us in touch with our inner world and deepens our own wisdom.

My own process of transformation, gave me a new lens in which to view the world, taking my fragmented monkey mind energies and flipping my own light switch on 360 degrees for living, loving, and healing in the present moment, in my first book, Beyond Gratitude. The crazy lady inside all the layers, too afraid to reveal herself in totality.

I used to be afraid of feeling! Now I shout, 'bring it on!' Mindfully of course.

This is what encapsulates living in the light to me: To live simply and freely, to eat chemically free food, to openly hug another and feel loved, to have the basic right to clean water, to express our creativity naturally, without feeling subjective to that old chestnut of, I'm not good enough. To choose what you want and will put into your own body, because it is your choice. A choice of free will. Of informed consent. Of weighing up the pros and cons from your own internal experience. Of living, breathing and being exactly how you are meant to be without projection, guilt, or fear. Fear is an illusion. Only love is real, that is our gift of creation. Light is our gift of information. I have heard some lovely people call light our imagination. If you can imagine it, then it can come true. If you really know how to get out of your own way and receive, that is mastery. And another thing, why would you want to dumb down all the little miracles and magic of aliveness that each moment by moment, with awareness, can bring? Why sedate that?

That's pure Sacrilege to our higher selves. A famous American comedian once said that 'praying' is talking to God and 'schizophrenia' is when God talks back to us.

On extension, Jesus said, "You are light for the world" (Matt 5:14). Signifying that we carry his light within us and are responsible to illumine the truth of Christ to others.

Shine on.

Twin flames

Right let's get stuck right in. Some of you will perceive this to be a true reality. Some of you might not have heard of this phenomenon and will be scratching your head, others will sit on the fence. So, here's my perception, drawing from many realms.

Incidentally, I used to perceive truth in this so-called Twin Flame connection as I have experienced this push – pull partner dynamic myself, where the link was phenomenally intense. I'd never felt that way before, ever in my life, and this feeling was tremendously seducing while exhilarating, but I didn't comprehend it at the time. I was bathing in the esoteric fancifulness of feeling deep romantic love, and divine connection. I'd never felt the experience of intimacy or anything like it before. Ever! After 20 years married, living in prescriptive cohabitation, I'd felt like I'd been living in the dark ages with my sexual, creative expression and I was completely seduced, mesmerised, plus hypnotised as the spark within, enflamed into a greedy raging inferno of insatiability. I became blindly hooked.

Here's why.

In spiritual terms this is what is banded about in this New Cage paradigm. The Ascension Journey of Twin Flames.

In briefish terms:

144,000 illuminated twin flames have been incarnated on the planet earth to aid humanity during global ascension.

They're called illuminated twin flames because these beings can hold a higher frequency of light than any other being inside a dense human body.

Photon and gamma light beams are reaching Earth, piercing the cells of every living organism.

The beings who can integrate this light first, are the enlightened ones, enabling others to access this light energy.

144,000 is the number allowed by the alliance, ensuring that the free will of mankind is not violated.

There are other beings of light and more twin flames incarnate now.

The 144,000 were just one of many waves of highly evolved beings that were sent to Earth to fulfil one of many special tasks.

Over the past few years, many twin flames have been reunited.

It's a rare feeling of indescribable love, with an unprecedented depth that surpasses one when they meet their twin flame.

It feels like the fulfilment of an inherent desire to become one with another, even if you didn't know you had this kind of desire before you met your twin flame.

With the completion of Earth's ascension to the fifth-dimension frequency, a photon belt will spread around our planet.

This belt will protect the spatial and temporary reality of our planet from being attacked again by any other species.

Other planets also have similar protective light belts. That's why when humans land on a planet they find nothing there.

You need to have the right coordinates to enter through the space-time portal if you want to visit and see another alien civilisation.

This photon belt will bring thousands of years of peace to Gaia, where Earth's species can live and thrive in Earth's 5D sky.

The twin flames have agreed to come into this realm during this time of drastic change and go through the immense pain, drama and, most importantly, the process of amnesia to meet and reunite with their divine counterpart.

It's the love these beings have for each other that helps rebuild the earth's photon belt.

This planet is learning that the unconscious way humans lived life has not served them well.

Humanity is waking up to the truth that its ways are no longer sustainable and that the systems they've built, believed in, and protected are being destroyed in front of their eyes.

As the planet goes through an immense phase of mass awakening, Earth's peoples understand the role sexuality played and, more importantly, its distortion in their slave game.

As more and more people learn about Satanism, in which a limited and broken form of sexuality played an important role, everyone begins to question their own sexuality and, little by little, the way it was considered and practiced, sexuality is changing.

Sexuality is the most sacred and powerful act of spirituality.

It's what connects you to the divine, activates your Kundalini energy that runs through your 12 Chakras system and ultimately awakens your Crystical Consciousness. That's what the climb means.

When sacred sex is performed by twin flames, fully heart-centred and conscious, by two ancient lovers who worship each other like gods, the couple emits powerful beams of energy that repair the photon belt.

And yet more ... The love they create within their relationship makes this frequency of love accessible to other beings.

It raises the vibrational level of the earth and all its sentient life.

Often, twin flames have been infiltrated in various ways by dark leaders who wish nothing more than to stop the ascension of humans.

There may be emotional traumas, addictions, relationship damage, financial problems, physical distance, and many other problems that can, and must, be overcome to fulfil the divine plan.

It's the purpose of their life, their soul's mission, their Dharma.

If you've always wanted someone you can trust and love so much that you can lose yourself in them, you have a twin flame.

The encounter of twin flames is imminent.

Their union is part of the divine plan.

What's more, this type of relating is far greater than the soul mate, life partner, or karmic partner dynamic. According to those that 'know.' This is the ascension kind. Wasn't I the lucky one! Are you too?

Right, re-read the last page again. Where did this information come from? What source? Where is it detailed and documented? By what tribes? What scholars? Does it feel true? Where do you feel this truth in your body? If it is found on Google does this mean it is 100 percent true, and fact checked by whom?

I invite you to become the witness as you re-read it again, then read my version. When I say become the witness, imagine that you are the cameraman (or camerawoman) behind the lens and are simply noticing the words, without attachment or judgement, from a neutral space of simply observing.

Having been hoodwinked into perceiving this type of relationship to be true by the spiritual community, I dared to think that my Twin Flame would ever really leave me because he was my divine other half. I had a fear that this would be my only chance at 50+ years to meet someone and feel truly alive, in the highs and lows of it all, with another who completely stretched me on all levels. Don't forget I was a married women for many years, living in the comfort zone. I completely fell for this exciting trap. I was ensnared in the false reality of knowing, and being told from others, that my type of experiencing with this man in the spiritual community was true. It was a believed perception. No different than perceiving that Santa Claus or the Easter Bunny is real. I wanted transcendence. Whatever that meant.

Upon reflection, here's my more honest, experiential account:

So, I'm now 6 years divorced after 20 odd years together with the same man. My life includes proudly raising 2 very awesome children, now big people thriving in the world and I'm about to be a Nana.

For me, I had to go through the 'Twin Flame' phenomena, why? It appears that most humans do in some capacity in order to return to love. Sounds mad but feels true to me in self-development terms.

Upon reflection, I was vulnerable, I was not whole, I was grieving the loss of many of my family members, and I was grieving the loss of a life that I had known. I was a troubled woman, living in a troubled mind with an equally disturbed overweight and boozy body, wracked with pain from my own unresolved trauma. I was not ready for an intense relationship. Yet, somehow, the universe flung me an almighty, atomic, growth bomb to swiftly navigate, and one in which I was totally spellbound by. One that made me feel safe and simultaneously unsafe. Unsafe to really feel, express myself, speak, think, and feel emotionally validated. In-fact, towards the last few months before the relating took a nosedive, we both realised that this relationship had to move form for both our individualised growth. I began to feel as though I was treading on eggshells and trapped inside a little glass box in which I could see no emergency escape. I felt overwhelmed, crushed, and controlled by the smallest of things such as choosing food, restaurants, places to go or furnishings that I wanted. Just what had I become? What had I allowed in the name of a Twin Flame ascension and true love?

The only one that you will ever be blessed to have, if you believe the neigh slayers. No matter how intelligent you are, it is easy to be blinded by alchemical love when you are so needy. Yes, I feel ashamed to write this, but I was. I was fucking needy. I wanted so much to feel adored. I needed to feel desired and sexy. I wanted to play out all my messy parts and I loved that my TF brought out the adventurer in me, the wild spirit animal. And I really loved that. Or did I? Was I merely addicted to the adrenaline of the bad boy image? I had never clamped on a man before or given him a purple penis from passionate love making. Funnily, we had to wait several minutes until the intensity had passed so that we might unplug. We were glued together like dogs on heat. We both wished that we had taken a trophy photo in token memory. In Orissa, India, according to Verrier Elwin, the vagina dentata is known as the ferocious orifice of the wind that not only mutilates men but gobbles up the rice crop. I'd turned into Kali, the mother of all she demons, the goddess warrior triumphs in her castrating vagina as well as the swords she wields. Freaking intense. Have you nearly cut a penis off and died right there in the hammock?

During our love making, I was adept to passing out and disappearing into the black stillness of the cosmos, for quite some quivering time. I could be present in my body while out of it at the same time, experiencing no shape or form, just a knowing in the eyes of darkness. My TF intuitively knew what to do, he is a tantric, charming, and sublimating man, he'd cover me with a soft but weighty blanket to ease my pulsating. He would keep a careful eye on me until I had come around from my altered state. He would then place glass of water at my bedside and encourage me to sip my water frequently upon my bodily return.

Let me tell you some more.

It was not until after the 4th fatal incident that I truly acknowledged my part in all of this. I asked myself, just what am I allowing here. I am going to be vulnerable and honest with you now. These are stark situations that I found myself forgiving. Over and repeatedly, again and again, did I repeat this sympathetic pattern until I started to gain clarity within the context. There are many harsh reality check memories. Yet, I do not need to go into the gory details of them, otherwise I'd be writing an encyclopaedia.

Am I sad? Not at all, I have learnt to be grateful for all of it because without the experiences, I would not be writing to you now, as I just wouldn't have the knowledge. The direct experiential types. The richest stuff. Shamefully, to the detriment of other women, I own this. These were sharp events from the universe to 'wake the fuck up.' Delivered ever so sweetly from my 'apparent' beloved TF. You will note that this took me many painful lessons to finally get it. Have you experienced this too?

Previously, I have been gaslit when explaining my feelings of hurt. Well, it's all about me again. No, I'm telling you how I feel my love. It is not for you to feel sorry or react, it's up to me to decide how I react, it's your choice how to respond. This is information that wants validating that's all. To be heard, nothing more to do other than finding the middle way of acceptance.

Sadly, we are not taught about these things from an early age in school. It is not embedded in any curriculum. But saved for later life when life crumbles. And why? Why stuff the brain with only cognitive intelligence, factual statistics, then ostracise the more emotionally intellectual children by lowering their self-esteem, by not teaching a balanced curriculum, one that includes self-enquiry, emotional development, self-love, or even entrepreneurialism. We wouldn't need to seek therapy in later life if the self-enquiry seeds of understanding were planted earlier on in a child's developing mind.

Life is about acceptance and finding the gifts.

Why yes, I have broad shoulders to know that behind anger, there is pain, sadness, and bitterness but as I have said before, there is only so much you can take before your own mental and physical health deteriorates, you must close the door and let the universe do its job with the highest intention of love. It always brings us back to love.

Karma says that when somebody is not right for you, God will continuously use them to hurt you until you are ready to let them go.'

Ouch, that hurts.

Life is too short and precious to hold any resentment, anger, or bitterness in the body. It will cripple you in later life and will rob you of your ability to notice all the wonder, magic, aliveness, love, and beauty of the present moment. The only place of eternal power. I know this to be true from my own story. The power of the now.

So, what is this crazy lady embarking on nowadays?

In a nutshell, I've hopefully completed my very physical, mid-life crisis, mental breakdown, spiritual awakening or whatever it is you want to call it. Thank God, after 6 tedious years, that mystical material has moved through me. I've worn the spiritual guru white clothes and wooden beads and prayed to Shiva, squirted my eyeballs out to Shakti, drank my wee, silenced the hell out of silent retreats, connected with the holy mother Ayahuasca, gazed on the terrace on many a rooftop hotel, eyes gazing up at the stars, wondering who is out there and fasted until my ribs look like a xylophone. Are you with me so far? I'd try absolutely anything to distract myself or heal myself from the pain I was feeling in my body mind. What is more is that I did that in a time frame when travelling the globe was free and unlimited!

Yet, I am still bound by the challenges of family life and living. No change. Or has there been? Let's see.

Thankfully, I have exhausted all the traps of being able to transcend the body into an altered state of consciousness, in which I could reframe that as escapism via the spiritual teachings, and practices like non-duality. I have come to see this as another trap. No wonder spiritual teachers do not live in the UK and vacate to more liberal climates where there is no accountability for real people's lives. In Europe, I've seen a woman, heartbroken and in tears when told to drop all attachment by her spiritual guru, when she clearly just wanted to share her story, her experience of who she is, what makes her and what she was suffering with.

Yet, at the start of my own journey, I really did perceive that I was lacking in the spiritual department, the spirit side of ourselves. Now, I have come to realise this as non-self-love. How can anyone really love another without truly loving thyself first? Impossible.

What else have I come to know?

Most humans will do anything to escape from the truth. From the bare reality of the boringness of it all. Many fill their lives with boozy nights, sugar loaded treats, heavy carbs, Netflix, mind-numbing boring conversations, porn, gambling, and whatever else distracts them from sitting in the nothingness of life. There is absolutely nothing to do at all unless you are using these devices to stuff down your emotions to prevent your trauma wounds coming up, and your unconscious mind is driving your self-sabotaging behaviours.

On the flip side...

With awareness, when you are being the inner work, life is in the simple pleasures, in the senses, the scent of a rose, the shades of an iridescent night sky, the touch of a loved one, the laughter through connection. The greedy pig whose face lights up with a bloody, mooing steak and fries, or the satisfaction you get from cleaning your windows. Well maybe not that for you if you are vegan, but do you get my drift? Life is in the daily bumping and grinding and if you get to do that with a cherished one whose values, morals and energy matches yours, and you've cleared your inner wounds with kindness, then you've hit the jackpot. That is living rich. Does this make sense to you?

Are you ready to feel these words in your own heart? They are offered as walls of support if you are considering going on a yoga retreat in a tropical location.

Sisters, will you honour your sacred sanctuary? Your church? Your beautiful yoni?

Do you love yourself fully? Or will you allow the bubble of illusion to distort your integrity and authority?

Yes, we are one but also very separate, housed in very single divine vessels, with very different conditioning, patterns, projections and stories blah, blah, blah.

But do not be fooled into sharing your most holy sanctuary with another, in terms of trauma healing, for kundalini or for enlightenment. Stay safe, even with a teacher or elder. You are most vulnerable and beautiful and should respect, honour and value your holiness in sharing/talking to anyone. To be safe share with a female, elder, wise Shakti and take a friend with you for support. Do not be drawn into the false guru healer.

Remain cautious:

Do the teachers at the school have a CRB check? Is their work monitored? By whom? Are your needs as a student, and as a sacred flower, held securely for growth and expansion? I know from experience that trauma, held and stored in the womb, comes up a lot for women in these environments. We are the power houses over the masculine because we have the life force within our wombs. We need to be treated sensitively and without illusion.

Please stay centered. Do not fall into a false delusional world of shallow, physical feelings for strangers, for the sake of healing? Who is healing who exactly? The ego manipulator at getting their desires filled. Do you know if your intimate connection has any STI that you know about? As a woman, type 2 herpes can damage your chances of fertility. Think of the consequences, if this is not your beloved, because you need to understand that because you are affecting your future not healing it. Nor as a woman will you be going into your own power by taking this way for healing.

It's so immoral and it will only end bad for both of you. You need to know this. I hear it so much and the men that then say, 'Oh I needed to heal her.'

Fair enough when there isn't another soul involved but be careful that you aren't being manipulated. Healing her and destroying her? Where is the exchange in that?

So, as a highly conscious person who is working on the inner clearing work, you naturally are aware of how important it is to keep your energy fields clean.

There is a deep love for oneself and the Divine, with a deep respect for all of life and most of all, a respect and love for one's own physical, emotional, and mental state. This is crucial to understand. If male and female just merge for the sake of play, and there is no understanding of the sexual energy; the energy is used for self-gratification purposes only.

However, the sacred union between 2 souls, is a deep and profound love and honoring of the other and in perfect DEEP TRUST. In essence, it is the act of Creation itself. It brings a type of beautiful energy between the 2, that forms a deeper and more profound bond of love, for it is done with immense love and with the heart wide open.

In divine union between 2 souls, you also become aware, that your most beautiful and profound powerhouse within you, your sexual organs, are a profound energy sanctuary that you honour and care for.

Just like would not just let anyone trample all over your house with muddy boots on; you would not just allow anyone into your inner sanctuaries to share your most beautiful manhood/womanhood with. Would you?

I would not solely ask the question, 'Who am I?' But would also contemplate, "Do I love myself?" Do I understand fully the consequences of 'plugging in' with another for play or healing?

Beautiful Goddesses' we have experienced enough pain and if we are to support the masculine, we need to fully personify into the reality of conscious loving relationships. We need to help them by embodying in totality, our self-respect for our most holy sanctuary between our divine hips, with full awareness. Just thinking about the implications of the various manifestations after insensible DNA, cellular energy exchange, makes me shudder. Do you really want to absorb the energy of the other on so many levels?

I have a very beautiful daughter, and granddaughter.

No more words.

What the fuck?

There are many alleged trials and tribulations about the founder of the Thai-based yoga and tantra school, Swami, has been accused by multiple women of sexual assault. He claims to be the "brilliant exponent of a unique and modern trend of thinking in Yoga" who "has reached high states of spiritual realisation." This school is one of the world's largest yoga training centres. Swami's teacher, the infamous Romanian yoga guru Gregorian Bivolaru, was sentenced to six years in prison for having sex with an underage girl after being wanted on Europol's Red List for sexual exploitation of children and child pornography.

According to Europol, he acted as his underage female victim's spiritual mentor and used this power to sexually abuse the girl. To repeat the acts, he gave the girl various amounts of money and other benefits.

Swami warns those who dare to speak against him that they are under "demonic influence" and face "infernal consequences for many lives to come." Several of his most senior teachers have also been accused of rape or sexual assault.

The website also promotes courses in other 'alternative' workshops including "Kundalini, Bhakti, Nidra, and Raja Yoga(s), The Tibetan Book of The Dead, Astrology, Psychotherapy, Rebirthing, Metaphysics, and much more".

Wow was he …! (Better than a three-headed dog. Or the three Holy Heads of John the Baptist. Somebody must be selling it on Ebay.

What are the principles of these teachings based upon? What is the historical pedagogy? The art of seduction?

The website makes no mention of the allegations against the centre or changes made to avoid further abuses, after notorious journalist Be Schofield lifted the lid on his scrutable antics in 2018 about his noble, and charming teachings.

Wearing my schoolteacher hat, the pedagogy in most parts, is rather deliciously fascinating, but is it tarnished with perversion? One can understand the desires to get closer to this type of character. Knowledge and wisdom are very attractive qualities and energetically alluring in another. It can be seducingly so because you are so vulnerable and crave so much. Some deep wounds inside long for drastic change.

In one allegation, Ana Smith, the mother of a former yogi pupil, Deborah Topp, claims that in 2017, the Swami convinced her daughter not to return to Australia for breast cancer treatment and instead follow his natural remedies. These 'remedies' included eating only brown rice and drinking her own urine and menstrual blood, which she said he allegedly claimed to have used in the past to "successfully cure cancer".

The mother said that Deborah eventually returned to Australia three months later after the lump had grown rapidly. Despite a mastectomy, Ana says it was "too late" as the cancer had spread and "her chances of survival had long expired".

In the Catch 22 words of one of his former close disciples of many years, and the beloved brother with whom I shared a consecrated, and delicious awakening session:

'Narcissist could manipulate, because, while conducting my awakening sessions, I observed what was happening in the minds of a huge number of single, and not only single, women who are looking for truth in smart, and if you are lucky, then also in sexual, men.

Now, sister, it's clear who I often caught in my mind while watching the teachers at the schools, who consider themselves smarter, and more spiritual, than others, especially when they communicated with new students or female students. Seeing them admiring themselves, you laughed ironically so that my mind needed the support of my father to maintain restraint and the position of the observer.

Firstly, I did not believe, and still cannot believe, knowing him well enough, that a narcissist could rape by physical force. if that were the case, he would have been in prison a long time ago.

I knew that women themselves went to him for private conversations, and if he managed to exalt his mental charm, then he would gladly, fulfilling his lust-inspired teaching duty, lower this charm to the level of the second chakra, and diligently help them open their sexuality.

They tried to believe him at first, not expecting a dirty trick, and to someone, his divine magic even revealed everything that could be revealed, including sexuality.

But some, not having received the expected result, and feeling deceived, nevertheless decided to punish him.'

Anyways, after an initial consultation with a blonde female 'doctor 'on the tropical isle, I was informed that group sex participation was the antidote to overcome divorce. Can you imagine the look on my face when I was told that I needed to be 'fucking to God?' (the yoga schools' mantra)? Another unnamed girl's advice given from the centre was 'three men a day,' she said. Hurriedly, I made a swift exit.

> Fuck you and your energetic cock,
> You cannot drain me anymore,
> Light from my soul,
> You are toxic,
> My light is eternal,
> It will never be dimmed,
> It will never heal the depths of your dark soul or history,
> I bless you with my crystal heart mind,
> All is forgiven,

I live on in the light even more,
Thank you, dark wisdom,
I enable no more.

Nonetheless, go check out Yogi Bhajan, or John of God too. Do some research beforehand in your quest for truth, as certain, so called 'spiritual masters' have thousands of followers, some of which have been 'healed' by the alleged experts. The universe and everything in it are comprised of atoms. Therefore, we shouldn't be surprised to learn that the kind of energy we transmit, and encounter, shapes our lives on multiple levels. Arguably, we have a responsibility to discover as much as possible about human energy transfer and how it may be harnessed for the greater good. Although the effects of other people's energy may seem like common sense, it has taken mainstream science a long time to investigate this occurrence. Are we really the average of our 5 closet friends?

Meanwhile, back in the land of the known territory, I remained curious enough to want to find out more on how the cervix hid the stories of our DNA and past lovers. And how, with a specific type of yoni massage, stored trauma can be released and healed. Catch 22. When you have a tooth problem you go to the dentist and the dentist will remove the tooth. Voilà. But when you are working with the energetics of the body, that which the mind cannot see, but feel, we are talking on another level and there are so many lightworkers, healers, and bodyworkers out there, but are we are opening ourselves up to being made vulnerable and taken advantage of?

Yes, I know there is good and bad in everything, in every profession and walk of life but if you are a highly sensitive person who has experienced trauma, discerning can be tricky. Believe you me, it is so hard to distinguish as you cling to the desire to want to feel whole again or normal. I mean, seriously normal again. Whatever normal means.

Looking back, was I really fucking screwed up? Or was I learning some remarkable characteristics about being a woman? About how incredibly resilient and giving we are as a species? How much do we give to allow another to feel the depths of our compassion? What if the man had had a wounded life and you are playing the rescuer? For that helps to feel wanted and needed? To fit any missing jigsaw puzzle pieces. Can you understand this? Our intuitive, healing womb of spirit gives us the expansive capacity to give endlessly. This is aligned with Mother Nature, as she gives endlessly and mercifully too. Open your eyes and look for yourself.

So, what is the big, enlightened issue? What is it that I have come to believe?

Are old chains, those deeply embedded heavy chains, only smashed apart through painful experiences? Through deeply loving and moving experiences with our powerful mirror lovers that reflect physical, mental, spiritual, and emotional expansion? Acknowledging trauma responses which include defensiveness, aggression, freeze mode, checking out, dissociating, and full-on emotional disconnection? From a nervous system response?

Tah dah…

Ladies, when trust or respect is spoiled, and only an insane sexual chemistry is offered, which you perceive to be alchemical, is there a foundation to build on? Is having great sex a lasting bond?

If your hearts cannot meet and merge, is there a point? Nor do I advocate that there is a wrong person methodology and a right. That one is good, while the other is bad. No.

That is not what I am saying. We are different expressions of human forms.

At the end of the day, as in most relationships, they involve 2 traumatised people, trying their upmost best to navigate this thing called life. But without trust and respect, love alone cannot survive in the jungle.

There is an old Cherokee who is teaching his grandson about life:

"A fight is going on inside me," he said to the boy." It is a terrible fight, and it is between two wolves. One is evil – he is anger, envy, sorrow, regret, greed, arrogance, self-pity, guilt, resentment, inferiority, lies, false pride, superiority, and ego." He continued, "The other is good – he is joy, peace, love, hope, serenity, humility, kindness, benevolence, empathy, generosity, truth, compassion, and faith. The same fight is going on inside you – and inside every other person, too."

The grandson thought about it for a minute and then asked his grandfather: "Which wolf will win?"

You might hear the story ends like this: The old Cherokee simply replied, "The one you feed."

In the Cherokee world, however, the story ends this way:

The old Cherokee simply replied, "If you feed them right, they both win." and the story goes on:

"You see, if I only choose to feed the white wolf, the black one will be hiding around every corner waiting for me to become distracted or weak and jump to get the attention he craves. He will always be angry and always fighting the white wolf. But if I acknowledge him, he is happy, and the white wolf is happy, and we all win. For the black wolf has many qualities – tenacity, courage, fearlessness, is strong-willed and great at strategic thinking – that I have need of at times and that the white wolf lacks. But the white wolf has compassion, caring, strength and the ability to recognise what is in the best interest of all.

"You see, son, the white wolf needs the black wolf at his side. To feed only one would starve the other and they will become uncontrollable. To feed and care for both means they will serve you well and do nothing that is not a part of something greater, something good, something of life. Feed them both and there will be no more internal struggle for your attention. And when there is no battle inside, you can listen to the voices of deeper, knowing that will guide you in choosing what is right in every circumstance.

Peace, my son, is the Cherokee mission in life. A man or a woman who has peace inside has everything. A man or a woman who is pulled apart by the war inside him or her has nothing.
"How you choose to interact with the opposing forces within you will determine your life. Starve one or the other or guide them both."

-Cherokee Story

Then think about this question, which wolf are you feeding? Is one of them getting a bigger meal? Upon whom is the accountability placed? Who is doing the safeguarding? Historically, perpetrators are men. At the hands of men, many women have suffered enormously in many ways.
Women, how many of you are reading this and have suffered at the hands of men?
To those who have endured any such emotional, physical, mental, or spiritual pains, I trust you are free and living in peace now. I love you.
I am not advocating shame on any man. Trauma is ancestral and complex. Teal Swam sums up what I want to say perfectly:

'That you cannot heal shame, with more shame and disconnection, nobody commits crimes on another unless they are disconnected from who they are committing them on. We need to find a way to bring them back into society. We need to reconnect with them.'

However, my question to you is this, what does this say about our current patriarchal society. Is it balanced and fair? How can we live in an age of information, but not have the emotional intelligence and skill set to rectify this abuse? It's historical, outdated and certainly not in line with current trends of unity, of love, of sharing is caring, in the great minds of the higher consciousness and evolving beautiful new world?

The solution to healing from abuse, is not teaching the survivor to forgive. The solution is holding the abusers accountable, so the abuse stops. This is the message that needs to be passed on to the next generation, so that abusers have consequences, rather than enablers.

This is asking you to take the biggest risk imaginable.

There is a well-known saying…

'Fool Me Once, Shame on You; Fool Me Twice, Shame on Me.'

I believe that in all of life there is a spectrum on everything. In the case of the TF, you can call it Narcissist relating if you like. I do sometimes. Similarly, this could be complimentary to opposite polar energies between partners. Empath versus Narcissist. To somehow balance the extreme nature of each other, to somehow find middle ground. Does this make sense? Let me add that I am not stating that having narc tendencies is bad. One must dive into the childhood experiences to establish the adult patterning and then join the dots to see where the friction between the 'downside' aspects of the relating lie. Have we ever been told this? Narcissism itself connotates a negative energy. What if we learnt to look at the positives in a relationship and focus on that instead of the mind directly flowing to the negatives, the dark stuff? What if we learned about our own unique behaviours so that we might harmonise and uplift another, strengthening the relationship knowing and honouring the diverse value?

Either way, it is an opposing force of nature that has so much wisdom and information in it, if you are able to drop everything and look closer. That is, if you too are in or have experienced this type of intense connection.

I know I'm a deeply sensitive person who feels everything, I always have. On a scale of 1-100. I believe my TF has about 58 precent narc tendencies. He is not a full-blown psychopath (joking), but his mission in life is that. To blow apart other misconceptions.

He is the wandering nerve, the vagus nerve manifestation of a powerful man. Is this a 'bad' attribute? I've inherited a score of 43 per cent, no one gets out alive. Take the free narcissistic personality disorder test online and find out instantly if you have it. It's quick, free, and confidential and you'll get your results quickly. Could be designed by a Psychopath too. There is always a black and a white wolf to feed. Am I therefore, a dark empath?

"Women, we are not rehabilitation centres for badly raised men. It's not your job to fix him, raise him, parent him, or change him. You want a partner, not a project."

Julia Roberts

Without this so-called TF experience in my life, I would not have fine-tuned my bullshit or finely tuned love radar. It is only mine though, unique to me of what resonates and what doesn't. I choose. I most definitely needed to go through the process, despite being weak and vulnerable, to level up, so to speak. Not in a masculine way, but in a soft and intuitive feminine way. This relating has finally given me a measure of what I do want and accept in my life. I am now in a place to feel blessed by it. I hope you can say the same.

Albeit I'm still at the releasing stage and this feels unbearable, as if a knife is cutting through my whole physical being like a lump of raw meat, and then twisting it around as I roll about on my stinky sweaty bedsheets for 2 whole days. I seem to do this a lot. It is not a glamourous or enjoyable experience either. It makes my body and bedclothes stink like parmesan cheese. It churned up my dark shadow side, the one that wanted to die. Both my grandmothers committed suicide at my current age, and I now know how they felt, mixed with the hormone imbalance of menopause, fuck, it's a heady cocktail. Thank God that I am an experienced meditator, as I am able, through puffy, red slit eyes, to witness the whole damn lot like clouds passing in the sky. By the way, one killed herself through an overdose on prescription tablets despite failed EST, the other by suspended hanging. Both early 50's. Bless them shall we, and all other women who bravely opt out.

God bless my TF too. If that was really what he was/is. I wish him nothing but the best in his next adventure, sharing wake-up calls with other much-loved souls, in the name of God and growth. Or will he? Or have our goal posts moved into a new way of relating so that the much-needed space is given, to allow what wants to happen, without labels? And for the magnificence of our beings, in separate homes, to expand and fly? Had I been struck once again in the comfort zone of being looked after and cared for by a man. Did I lose trust and respect for myself? Was this what was being reflected to me by the purposeful, big, ballsy man whom all of life sings through in his own truth? Was Sarah slowing down with menopausal age, and he speeding up? Or do I just ruminate too frequently? Or would you say that my terms of reference are a bit of a muddle?

I feel you asking me this question. Did you try to talk to him about it all? Yes, of course I did, we did, we even tried Relationship Therapy but even that was of little use. I couldn't stop howling tears while my whole-body shook, he did not acknowledge any of it, or even give me a supportive hug as he was suffering with a neck strain. It is all about his needs. Could I clearly communicate mine? Was I stuck in freeze mode again? Did I feel safe enough to express myself without feeling like I was treading on eggshells? Enough said. Have you ever felt like this too?

One of the most iconic, and disturbing, scenes in Glenn Close and Michael Douglas' 1987 thriller, Fatal Attraction, is when Anne Archer comes home and discovers her daughter's rabbit boiling in a pot of hot water. It's an absolutely shocking moment that highlights Alex's (Close) extreme obsession with Dan (Douglas) and her desire to win him back at any cost. Ring any bells? Was I a bunny boiler?

In the reality of the TF phenomenon, had I met the male equivalent of myself, my very own black mirror opposite? A fucking scary and head wreck process.

Twin flame or trauma bond? More recent research shows that the bonding occurs because we can become addicted to the hormonal and emotional rollercoaster our partner puts on us. Kati Morton, licensed therapist, advocates that even if the abuse is bad, the love and attention you get afterwards feels good to the point that it makes you forget. She also states that your brain can get used to the 'ups and downs of it,' that you start craving it. The rush of the stress hormone cortisol mixed with the feel-good chemical dopamine, triggers the reward centre in our brain which causes you to perceive that you are in love with your partner. Interesting, eh? Does this sound like a TF relationship? A push pull, predator prey, type of relating? One in which you feel stuck in the relationship, and if you do try to leave, you feel an intense desire to see that person again. The pain of that longing will always bring you back. It is difficult to break this cycle, but so is any addiction, don't you agree? Even if at times you feel like you are walking on eggshells or might say something to set them off. Even if you know they are doing hurtful things to you, leaving is difficult because you are afraid, they may hurt you, or themselves.

In the words of Dr Omari,

'The motivation for trauma bonding can feel like love because you are so attached to this person regardless. You are validated by your partners approval.'

Who else couldn't tell their friends or family because you knew they would be disturbed by some of the things that your partner has done or said to you? So, you play it down and don't make a big deal of it?

Who else has had friends tell them about their concerns but you pretend to not know what they are talking about?

Have you broken the cycle of this type of relating too by being honest with yourself, by setting boundaries? Did you find it very hard to do too? Did you end that relationship successfully and work on you? Did you seek out specialist help with a trauma focused therapist?

Amen and thank you my darling TF, Narcissist or trauma bond partner in crime or whatever blend of cocktail aligns with your own soul. In hindsight, I look back with fondness on our journey together with gratitude. I'm just an old, sentimental, hormonal, soppy sod.

Do I believe we transcend with this type of connection? That we should stay with this type of partner for the rest of our life? For the sake of our correlation and togetherness? As prescribed? Who even thinks all this?

No. I believe that they come to us for a reason. To heal and discover something so profound within us that is the gift. To heal scars which you cannot see with the physical eye like you can with a bruise.

Are they scars or incredible life lessons, ones that you couldn't possibly read from a book? Or attain a magnificent purple member? I'll allow your imagination to work that one out. Right now, the darling Paula Yates and the charming Michael Hutchence romance springs to mind. Do you remember their first public encounter on The Big Breakfast cow print bed? Legs entwined? WOW! Undeniably, electrifyingly tangible with a saddening ending.

I know that some of this material is a tad harrowing, and believe me, at the time, I expressed every emotion you can muster. The whole messy lot, the energy in motion, full swing, full metal jacket range. From the darkest to the lightest shade to somewhere in between.

Currently, TF and I are in a state of allowing. Neither of us exactly know what we should call our relating energetically for the sake of those living in dense 3D matter bodies. Truth be told, we don't know either. We have incompatible traits that trigger us to lands' end. He wraps tons of toilet tissue around his hand when using the bathroom, and loves buying tons of useless gypsy nick knacks. This drives me insane. I am a minimalist. He turns all the lights on, I prefer the low dull tones. Petty, I know but when you are bumping and grinding with someone each day in partnership, rotating in life, in dense energy environments, it's easy to take each other for granted and start seeing more of those niggling characteristics than remembering the good because you forget to inspire each other. It's a tough slog whether you love someone and are attracted to them, or not.

We both understand our connection and are intellectually on par and are beyond grateful for every juicy moment of it, just as God, or whatever value works for you, loves us to believe. Whatever our soul-to-soul energetical connection is, I accept and thank the great wonder of the universe for that kindness. This relationship has taught me so much. It taught me how to not ignore my gut brain, I learnt how to love myself and not put anyone above my happiness and dreams. Now I know my worth, and know what I want, and I won't settle for less than I want again. No regrets, I needed to learn those lessons. Does this sound like you too? Do you recognise the gifts in your relating?

Love to you my awakening man.
Always and in all ways.

Darling, I'm here for you,
Darling, I know you are there,
For him, for her,
Happiness and suffering are inter-are
Mindfulness,

A lotus flower cannot bloom without dirt,
Meditation is living in the here and now,
For that is all there is,
Unless tangled up in the matrix,
In the ego, personality, monkey mind form of I,
Where is we?
Deeply listening develops a compassionate heart, which helps to heal our fellow man.
But touch, don't blend,
Release the tension from your body,
Create a feeling of joy,
Breathe the breath,
You are so very lucky,
There is no left shoe without a right,
No suffering, no happiness,
Mindfulness.
For him, for her...
Darling, I'm here for you
Darling, I know you are there
Darling, I know you suffer
Darling, I suffer too, I'm trying my best, please help me.
Darling, I love me, therefore I love all of you too
No suffering, no happiness
Mindfulness
Compassion is a flower of living elements
Generate the energy of compassion
Do you have the courage, or do you feel overwhelmed and keep running away from yourself?
Go home to yourself,
Put your phone down and rid yourself of the toxins of anger, shame, or guilt,

Great insight has the power to transform,
No suffering, no happiness,
Mindfulness,
Darling, I'm here for you.

P.S. No more gaslighting, enabling, hoovering, triangulation, flying monkeys, or any other play of the psyche ego unconscious conscious mind. If I spot this pattern again. Behold, I am fully aware of you now. I put up my protective shield and armour of self-love and walk on by.
I will send you love and blessings, but that is all. I know your little snake entrapments you dirty little rats. We see you and know your labyrinth mind games.

    Farewell my short-term buddies. You have expired your sell by date. Psychologists and psychiatrists and other 'mental health' professionals love to put a label on such terms so that the human mind can make sense of them and then project onto others. Remember the fingers pointing back at you?

    I will leave with this final thought. What if in child development, a certain part of the developing infant/child's brain is not fully activated in various parts relating to either cognitive or emotional intelligence? Perhaps you spent too much time alone in your bedroom with your thoughts? For example, you were shut down as an only child with very little stimulation and limited interaction with others. In turn not fully enriching and developing your empath limbic brain part. Just as an example, maybe this is just developmental and not negative as we have been designed to perceive. Maybe it's time to discover that those narc tendencies are not always destructive, but we need to find the middle way to find balance and compassion to those who have, for no fault of their own, but by design, experienced a different model of the world that shaped them. A different human pathway development which needs nurturing and understanding, not projecting, that it is wicked and cruel.

"There is a word in South Africa, Ubuntu, a recognition that we are all bound together in ways that can be invisible to the eye; that there is a oneness to humanity; that we achieve ourselves by sharing ourselves with others, and caring for those around us," Obama said.

"In this African Tribe, when someone does something wrong, they take the person to the centre of the village where the tribe surrounds him and for 2 days say all the good, he has done. The tribe believes each person is good but sometimes people make mistakes, which are really a cry for help. They unite to reconnect him with his good nature."

Nelson Mandela once said: "A traveller through a country would stop at a village and he didn't have to ask for food or for water. Once he stops, the people give him food, entertain him. That is one aspect of Ubuntu, but it will have various aspects."

Mandela is the true definition of Ubuntu, as he used this concept to lead South Africa to a peaceful post-apartheid transition. He operated with compassion and integrity, showing us that for us to be a better South Africa, we cannot act out of vengeance or retaliation, but out of peace.

Archbishop Emeritus Desmond Tutu, who led the Truth and Reconciliation Commission in 1996, also talked about the meaning of Ubuntu and how it defines us as a society.

"We think of ourselves far too frequently as just individuals, separated from one another, whereas you are connected and what you do affects the whole world," he said.
"When you do well, it spreads out; it is for the whole of humanity."

This is exactly what Ubuntu is about, it's a reminder that no one is an island, everything that you do, good or bad, influences your family, friends, and society. It also reminds us that we need think twice about the choices we want to make and the kind of impact they may have on others in our relationships.

There are no mistakes in this world. Even serial killers have a beating heart, and some abusers do feel remorse. Therefore, how can we collectively come together in unity, and apply more humanistic principles, with kindness, and compassion in our evolving new world, and turn the situation inside out and back to front then start to navigate this life through a higher collective, conscious, and crystal-clear, heart mind for our future generations?

Make up your own mind. Take accountability.

Mindfully feed your wolves.
If it's not feeling 100%
What's The Point?
Wild love.

Karma

Is karma a dish best served cold? Or sweet? Or Hot? Or in snippets? Or in big whacking truth bombs? Or as silent assassins? Or none of the above?

Anything unresolved within our energy field will keep manifesting itself in our physical, mental, emotional, and spiritual life until we heal it. There is no escaping this.

Are you in tune with and connected to yourself? Try these simple but crystal-clear heart-based questions to find out. Be honest.

Your time starts now:

* Did you exercise this morning? As simple as breathing, or walking? With full awareness?

* While taking the bath/shower did/do you thank water for washing your dirt or sweat? Thanking each part of your body in turn for working so cleverly for you?

* Did you worship to the GOD you believe in? Did you (always) ask or thank GOD!

* Was it easy to decide on what to wear for work or school?

* Did you smile at strangers or colleagues?

* Was your Office Desk or your surroundings clean? If not did you complain or try to make it clean?

* Did your work or you helping someone made a difference in the work?

* How was your 4 O'clock coffee or Tea? Did you take a healthy snack or dark chocolate with it?

* How does the checklist you prepared in the morning look? Is it 100% checked or 80% or 20%?

* Did you call your family to check if they want something on your way home?

* Were your family or pet (if you have one) excited to see you when you reached home?

* Did you shut down the excitement of your kids when they wanted to do something mischievous?

* Did you read something new today?

* Did you journal for the day?

* How many people did you tell that you loved them?

* How many hugs did you experience?

* Before going to sleep, did you thank everyone in your day for their love, including yourself for all the delights you had? Sleeping soundly with a clear and thankful heart?

Keep asking questions, smiling and if you answered YES to all.... you are living a very happy, present life and karma is your best friend. (Funny how I landed on 17 questions to contemplate on as my birthday is on the 17th!)

Well done. Keep this up and you will have a precious friend for life.

If not, open your heart, ask your experiences to take accountability and ask are they holding you back from this present moment? Are you constantly bringing in your trauma which will ultimately be blindly drawn into your reality?

Love cannot coexist with lies any more than the truth can exist alongside lies.

For all those men who say, "Why buy the cow when you can get the milk for free," here's an update for you. Now 80 percent of women are against marriage, why? Because women realise it's not worth buying an entire pig, just to get a little sausage.

My thoughts? Lean into life and become a veggie.

Thank you, my sense of humour, it's a credit to my Liverpool roots, renowned for quick wit. Ultimately obvious of course, however, I am now going through menopause and the hormone levels are dropping like pesky flies.

Change threatens our nervous system, but change also lies in the regulation and healing of that very same nervous system...... this is the paradox and exactly where the process begins...

Are you aware of your programmes and deep patterning that is engraved in your systems, influencing both your thoughts, words, and actions? That is, until you learn a new set because your subconscious mind/felt through your heart, knows that they no longer serve you? For example, deep down you have that knowing or inner itch that you really shouldn't have that 3rd glass of wine because you have a 'naughty head?' And you know the consequences! Yet, you want to quit booze altogether, but you just can't, it's a self-soother. Long-time friend? Your mother drank to relax, so you do too. That's normal behaviour.

However, you notice that are experiencing difficulties in certain areas of your body and its expression and don't know what to do? Your body is speaking to you telling you that your chakra system is blocked or under active. Maybe you suffer with throat problems and cannot speak your truth. Your heart is closed, and you cannot express love fully or receive it. Or, that you suffer with headaches or migraines due to crown centre blocks or have difficulty seeing your future self, or do not have intuitive insights as your 3rd eye represents fear of the unknown, poor concentration or focus too.

We are not educated in these tools. I never knew how to help my developing children express themselves properly in giving them the tools to say what their body needed for healing. Or what we could do about it to release all their emotions properly without judgement. I have never seen my adult son cry, yet, I have seen him angry.

Am I making sense?

Karma is a highly interesting construct, naked to the eye but felt and experienced subtly through the body mind, in circling spirals.

I'll allow you to contemplate on that for a few moments.

Kisses.

Magic

If you're not feeling 100%, what's The Point? Because if you didn't, you'd be missing out on all the magic and wonder that life brings to you.

This is my version on magic. In sparkly joy.

The universe is such a wild horse, passionately dancing in the ocean waves, shimmering blues of starlight, glittering bright hues across the horizon.

I miss the love of the ocean very much.

At sunset, the lulling that sends one into a blissful, deep sleep and at sunrise; it's joyous awakening laps from perfect slumber.

But the universe has spoken, if it's not feeling 100% true to the self, honouring the self, filling the self with desire, and igniting the flames of passion.

What's the point??

So dear friends, this harmonious time here has come to an abrupt close for now, in this magical part of the world in South America. The inner experiences fully absorbed and registered. The vibrational pull back to the UK is very strong

Karma Yoga is some more with the dear Mother Doris. After all, as a baby she patiently shared her understanding with me on how to use a spoon. The least I can do is help her to use an IPad, to connect with the wonders of technology, to support herself and feel less isolated. Plus, loving unconditionally of course.

My presence alone fills her with joy. And hers mine. She lives lonely, elderly, frightened and sick, masking a very beautiful soul that has hidden away from life for far too long.

Allowing a series of manifestation sickness to prevail instead. Misunderstood as a powerful woman and loving mother. Preferring the company of self-loathing alcohol that is John Smith to her true Godly self in her final years.

Nor does she understand that distance exists in the mind only, her heart does not feel this characteristic.

Consequently, I'm feeling re-energised, at home and comfortable with her projections, conditioning, patterning, and human emotions ... She loves them/it all. She feels no more processing, no more diving deeper, well at least not furiously on the self but rather in the gentle flow of things as and when they present themselves. And I love her dearly.

Finally, feeling satisfied or an inner calmness? It is hard to put into words really but feeling no more suffering and instead, a deeper yearning/readiness to serve.

What will she manifest next?

"There's nothing wrong with enjoying looking at the surface of the ocean itself, except that when you finally see what goes on underwater, you realise that you've been missing the whole point of the ocean. Staying on the surface all the time is like going to the circus and staring at the outside of the tent."

Dave Barry

Oh, the joys to live in the here and the now, to feel deeply into the unconditional joy and the dance of the wild horse freely. In love. In gratitude.

Your soul is pure energy and at this moment in time we are given a window opportunity to raise our own frequencies and vibrations, to become more in tune with the cosmic pulse.

Relationships in essence are not just about having great sex. Unfortunately, a lot of the hype these days is about having orgasms and gymnastic sex, about sex techniques, and whatever enhances performance. Sex is no glue to hold a relationship together. At some stage or other the little jackals appear, and the little jackals tend to grow into big ones, which eventually bite.

Most people (because of conditioned thinking and other factors), have little understanding of the sexual energy itself. The sexual energy, as all energy, does not need to manifest itself in PHYSICAL form. It is pure ENERGY. Thus, it vibrates, and has frequency and it can be used, like all forms of cosmic energy, for the greater good of all, or for self-satisfaction and self-service – or for destructive purposes.

So let us now, just for one moment, return to energy itself: Sorry for kicking back a gear into teacher mode again, force of habit I'm afraid but ...

The sexual energy at its very core, and as found within the Divine itself, is pure and is the life-force energy itself. It is a very beautiful and profound energy, that is meant to be used creatively and with immense love. The Male and Female parts of the Divine.

The two separate entities then have a third component and that is what is sometimes called the Holy Spirit. The three – male, female, and spirit essence, then form a sacred triad, which is the cornerstone, or foundation of all creation.

This is crucial to understand. If male and female just merge for the sake of play, and there is no understanding of the sexual energy, then this energy mostly is used for self-gratification. (WHAT CAN I GET OUT OF THIS?) It comes back to having the gymnastics for the sake of getting a kick out of the experience which can become like being addicted to that certain physical feeling that one gets, and one wants more of.

Modern society worships youth and its bodily form, without understanding that without maturity at SOUL level, the physical form is but a vessel and an empty one at that.

You have not got the wisdom and the insights into life when you are a teenager. That is a fact. One only grows into wisdom and maturity, as one goes through the school of hard knocks in life and starts delving deeper into the self. The rest is, but a futile attempt to find happiness in an act, that might give you a lot of physical sensations, but leaves you empty inside. There is no lonelier place to be, than lying next to someone in bed, and feeling the Arabian Gulf between two souls.

So, what is missing?

The soul and the third force, combined with a true understanding of the sexual energy force itself. Most of all immense and utter love + TRUST.

True awakening of the sexual energy comes with the true understanding of the energy forms and the way it manifests in our lives. Our chakra systems are in essence, energy wheels, as is every single vertebra of our spinal column. Most people do know about the kundalini energies, but have no understanding that the kundalini, is not in essence, the complete form of the sexual energy – it is one of those life streams, but not all of it.

WHEN THE UPPER AND THE LOWER COMBINE INTO ONE SINGLE FLAMING POWERHOUSE THEN THE COSMIC LAWS, AS ABOVE – SO BELOW, AS WITHIN SO WITHOUT, START APPLYING.

Now, we need to bring our physical energies in higher alignment with the Divine Energies. That means, when we raise our own consciousness and energy levels of the physical, emotional, mental and chakra bodies, we then start moving into a higher state of being. That means that all our chakras are fully opened.

The cosmic energies move through chakras into the crown chakras, then into the pineal and pituitary glands. I won't go into more than this because there is far more than this, and to try and do this without clearing the emotional charges and baggage accumulated over many lifetimes, and all the debris out of the sexual areas, it is such a shame, as some women's whole sexual area is one single scrambled mess of negative cords and attachments etc.

If, however, you have a deep love for yourself, the Divine, and a deep respect for all of life, and most of all, a respect and love for one's own physical, emotional, mental and all chakra bodies, then one starts to understand the sacredness of embodiment in form.

You also become aware, that your inner sanctuaries, that most beautiful and profound powerhouse within you, your sexual organs and pelvic bowl, are a profound energy sanctuary that you honor and care for.

Just like you would not just let anyone trample all over your house with muddy boots on. I've stated this before.

Nor would you allow just anyone into your inner sanctuaries, or to share your beautiful womanhood.

The more aware you become of the sexual energy, and the more you start to meditate on this, the more you will start understanding that the sexual energy itself is profound, and it is exquisitely beautiful. The more you start nurturing this flame from deep inside your own soul, the more you start to understand just how profoundly beautiful it is.

There is another something though- If you wish to reconnect with the sexual energy, first open your heart. Open your heart to love and allow love to flow into every single part and particle of your own body. Love yourself totally and in all that you are and aspiring to be. Become love in action.

Become the person that you would love to love and have an intimate relationship with. Love yourself past all the hang-ups, the fears, and stop beating yourself up.

How open is your heart? How would you love to be loved, and whom would you love to invite into those inner sanctuary of your innermost Goddess parts, and how would you love to receive him or her? Would that not be with utter trust and with so much love, and all your being opens to just receive, then lose yourself in the depth of your love and in all your being and soul?

When the act of sex, becomes an act of love and deep trust, it goes beyond the mundane, into the realms the Gods/Goddesses, the epitome of creation itself.

The beloved starts with you, self-love in action. With practice, it is possible to become so tuned in to yourself and become your own love guru.

Yes, love is made. It is not goal orientated, although having a full body orgasm for several hours can be most pleasurable. Only if the men in our lives knew! Shame, as they can only experience one, which usually results in rolling over and going to sleep.
Cultivating quality time to explore one another, will also help you slow down and feel into and explore your bodies needs more intimately. Plus, helping to draw up your sexual energy to move/shift or sublimate the energy around for healing purpose. Sounds confusing, I know, but thank you for bearing with me. All will be revealed soon, I promise.

Beautifully sadly, my Mum told me before she passed away, that my Dad was often too rough with her in bed, and she didn't enjoy sex much!! Little flower.

The time has come to reclaim and embrace our divinity, our creative power for the good of humanity.

Much juicy love to come. No pun intended.

If you want to change your thinking, heal your heart. That's the best meditation of all. (Spiritual Graffiti).

Although, a few years ago, my unhappiness wasn't caused by my thoughts; it was my undigested, emotional, Monkey Mind heart that was the issue. The resulting drama and chaos seeped up from my unclear heart and hence, the body suffered as a result.

So, to settle these ingrained responses in me and heal monkey hearts repetitive thinking to calm and clarify it, I took up several heartfelt practices for emotional release, deep charges, and full-blown heart openers. Meditation was vital.

Why?

Let me share my thoughts with you some more...

To get out of the head and into the heart space and to deeply feel into the body, I had to be still and quiet in silence. I needed to sit deeply in mediation so that I could feel the parts of myself that needed fixing, using the Chakra system as my guide.

Only when I had fine-tuned this mediation technique, was I able to devise practical techniques for me to heal on many levels. I had ignored my body and how it spoke to me for so long. It was time to start listening and paying full attention to my sacred body through my daily mediation practice. This was the key because intuitively, our bodies are designed to tell us how to heal and subconsciously, we do this but to be mindful and be fully present which is paramount to fully heal.

The chakra centres are like energetic motors within the mental/emotional/physical energy field we have. Each chakra centre relates to a different area of our body lives. The health of a chakra is governed by our beliefs about ourselves in the particular area of life that the chakra is related to.

For instance, the root chakra relates to our sense of connection with our fellow human beings, as well as survival issues. If a person believes they are unsafe and trust is difficult, this chakra will tend to be pulled in and not joined in harmony with the other chakras. This will affect the organs around the root chakra, such as the sex organs which can be under or over balanced and in women, can cause a wide range of manifestations. When I don't feel safe, this gives me an unbalanced root centre and I find myself manifesting disturbances in that department. Diarrhea or constipation anyone?

Energy flows where attention goes. Thoughts are powerful forms of energy. We all have experiences of reading each other's thoughts, such as having a song in your head and someone next to you starts singing it or knowing who is on the other end of the phone before answering it. The old way of looking at such things was that they are just coincidences. But as more and more of us are becoming aware of the true nature of our being - that we are Spiritual Energy Beings who are all connected - we now realise that we need to follow our own Inner Guidance rather than the ideas, rules, and restrictions, that in the past, society placed on us to follow. We are so much more powerful than we were led to believe. Where the mind goes, so does our creative power.

The woman/womb(man) is the womb for all of life, she is also the birth giver and the spiritual mother for this world. Therefore, it is essential that we get in touch with our divine feminine sexuality as this has a significant effect on our emitting behaviour to our children, family, partners etc. If she is weak, and unaware of her own joy, she will give birth to a world based on a collapsed feminine, and an over aggressive masculine, as we see today.

As a human race, we have never been taught the idea of letting go to these feminine principles, or if it is even safe to do so.

Women are Jewels.

And should be valued and cherished for BEing able to feel deeply and intuitively into life.

Who doesn't want to be honoured and cherished by a loving other, be held and seen and made loved to, in all the glorious forms of safe love making? Wild, sticky, hot, passionate, whore-like, gentle, soft, aggressive or with tears flowing? Yes, we women are often referred to as the moon, possessing as many faces as one.

To accomplish this, we must first love selfishly and with the deepest compassion, our divine selves. For how on earth can we love another human being, or express our sacred selves, explore, trust, feel safe with another if this is not so?

Pure cosmic, creative magic.

Resonates?

Embodiment

Embracing Life's Flow.

Today, it's Boxing Day, and the 10-year anniversary of my brothers passing from his suicide. Today I am releasing my love for him in a way that is energetically healthy for me, by symbolically placing flowers and a sharing a prayer to express my gratitude for his life and all that he enriched in mine.

Death and grief are traumatising enough when you lose a loved one, a very difficult process to fully accept and allow and let go of. Yet, in my experience this is something that can only be done gracefully in stages.

However, the energy flow, through your physical body, determines how it feels to live in your body, and we each have valuable parts, for the heart does not have an on/off switch, it doesn't know if a physical body is no longer around, it only knows how to feel.

For me now, at 3000 metres above sea level in the mountains of Peru, it feels like the final stage of letting go. For the first time it feels effortless. I have come to realise that when the energy is flowing through my body, I am releasing the old and welcoming in the new and healing happens effortlessly. In fact, that is what happens when the energy flows through your body: it gives rise to emotions ... emotions are the body's energetic release valve. Often, we are tempted to label this as a bad thing .... as something gone wrong. But when energy is flowing through your body, this is never a bad thing.

Change and flow and energy in motion is life.

The body giving rise to emotions and symptoms is a good thing, it is a natural way for your body to express what energy is flowing through it and to release it. This is what healing is all about, expressing the energy dynamic of the tissues, chakras, organ systems, emotional body and then releasing it.

Giving rise to symptoms is never the problem. Releasing it ... that's where it gets tricky.

Here are some tips on how to get into a state of allowing the energy to flow instead of resisting it. Here are ways to get more release, less resistance.

Sadness needs to physically flow through the body in order to release.

You must 'feel' the sorrow.

Don't try to resist it or put it off, instead get into the state of allowing the flow using this one simple trick: WATER.

Water is the ultimate medium of sacred flow on earth and comprises most of our body. In fact, water is the body's natural choice of release as well, in the form of tears or gushing. Both often help facilitate the flow of sorrow through the body and allows it to release more easily.

So, one tip is — allow the flow. Let the waters release your sorrow and lift it from your body. Can't cry or gush? You can still use the power of water to help facilitate the release of your sorrow, worry or grief.

* Use a hot water bottle full of warm water and hold it on your body where you are feeling the sorrow (chest, abdomen, neck, or back).

* Take a long hot bath (add some baking soda and apple cider vinegar to turn it into a detoxing experience).

* Sit in a warm shower and envision the water carrying your sorrow down the drain for you.

* Go for a relaxing swim or soak in a jacuzzi - my favourite is to take a wild plunge in a quiet lake.

* Use steam/humidifiers to help hydrate your head, clearing out the old mental fog and allowing room for the new.

* Drink water — hydrate, hydrate, hydrate, and hydrate some more during times of worry or sorrow, more than any other time of your life. Let your body be flushed out inside and out and with every urination or bowel movement recognise you are flushing the old energy down the drain and making way for new healing.

* A yoni steam works well to self soothe. I love using rose petals and geranium during mine.

I hope these tips help you to recognise that energy wants to flow through your body and be released. Honour the message. Getting into the state of release is the solution.

Did you know that…

"The first organ to form in the womb is the heart."

The Chakra system.

So, what exactly are the Chakras and why did a schoolteacher from the north of England begin to shift her logical brain and start to embrace them and, in the process, radically improve every aspect of her life?

Please let me return to being a teacher for a moment and present a short history lesson.

According to many traditional cultures, we have seven spinning wheels of energy running up and down the body from the base of the spine to the neck. These centres correspond to 'energy' centres of the main organs of the body.

The ancient Polynesians call this energy 'Mana' while Indian and Tibetan cultures call it 'Prana.' The Iroquis of North America call it 'Orendam', and the Chinese and Japanese call this energy Chi or KI.

Western medicine usually calls it nonsense.

OK, lesson over, I hope you were paying attention as there is a test at the end!

So how about you? Do you need to believe in the Chakra system?

This is how I see it …

Western medicine (and culture) is usually preoccupied with the brain, with thoughts, goals, plans and action. And it is here in the west that heart disease is out of control.

Jaw dropping levels of stress and depression in the west are also fueling massive profits for drug companies.

A traditional doctor can operate on the physical heart. But what about the esoteric heart that cannot be seen but from which sickness can manifest from the subconscious level due to stress, anxiety depression etc. along with all the other baggage that accompanies our 'more more more' western lifestyle?

Does more thinking help us to overcome these problems?

Like heartache from missing a loved one. Like my dear Mum. Perhaps you have someone in mind too?

Could we actually be thinking too much and feeling too little?

If we listen to Yoga teachers or reiki healers who live from the heart, we can learn that these energy centre can either be balanced as well as under or over balanced.

If we are simply able to be in tune with our bodies and read the signs that show up every day in our lives, we can master and selfheal ourselves.

It can be so simple to get in touch with this life energy. Keep reading and I will explain.

Just the other day I was in the Travel Agents, chatting to a lovely woman clerk who was complaining of a sore throat and was obviously irritable from lack of sleep.

After a short conversation, I asked her if she any trouble communicating her views, verbally, to any close family or friends?

Of course, she did! (Don't we all!)

She was experiencing a real drama between her son and his ex-girlfriend and their young toddler which was really affecting her emotionally as she didn't want to upset them by simply saying out loud what she needed to say.

I told her to speak from the heart exactly what she felt and that she would feel much better expressing her views, then her energy centre (in this case the throat chakra,) would then start to heal itself. Otherwise, if she didn't speak up, her manifested symptoms would persist and eventually become worse, possible developing to a throat infection or even tonsillitis.

I could immediately see and feel that her body language changed as she sat across the desk from me and how her gaze softened and that she had 'felt' with her heart what I had suggested.

She had begun the process of healing there and then and this was without actually sitting her son and his ex-girlfriend down and speaking to them!
It's clear that feelings and the heart are very powerful.

We use terms such as - she has a big heart or a soft heart or that we have had a change of heart. And when was the last time you told anyone that you love them with all of your brain!?

As I moved away from living in my own brain and towards living in my heart, magic started to happen. My health dramatically improved. My weight stabilised without any crazy western diet plan. My levels of creativity soared, and I have boundless energy and absolutely love my life.

How do you feel Right Now while you read this, what emotions and thoughts are coming up?

Read a little more about the symptoms of blocked energy in the body. This is how many eastern doctors see the patient:

1st Chakra (Root) – Do you feel grounded? Are you physically healthy?
2nd Chakra (Sacral) – Do you have abundance in your life? Are you an emotionally balanced person? Are you comfortable expressing yourself sexually?
3rd Chakra (Solar Plexus) – Do you have a high degree of self-esteem? Are you confident?
4th Chakra (Heart) – Do you have love in your life (friends, family or significant other)? Are you emotionally connected to others, and/or have a strong social network?
5th Chakra (Throat) – Do you communicate your thoughts to others well? Do people consider you articulate?
6th Chakra (Third Eye) – Do you intuitively just "know" certain things, without being taught beforehand? Are you wise? A deep thinker? Do you have a well-developed "mind's eye"?
7th Chakra (Crown) – Do you understand your spiritual connection to all that exists? Are you able to recognize your inner and outer beauty?

Did you answer "no" to many of the questions? It's ok if you did, most adults today, living in a head driven western culture, have at least few (if not all) blocked chakras!

Here is a simple method that is free and has been used for centuries to promote better health: Meditation

We will dive deeper into this topic next time but until then if you are still not feeling this concept of energy and living a heart led life try this –

Imagine you are introducing yourself to a deaf person… where do you place your hands when you mouth the words 'my name is' did you place them on your head, or over your heart?

"When you reach the end of what you should know, you will be at the beginning of what you should feel."

Kahil Kibran

If you thought sudoku and crossword puzzles were the only ways of exercising your brain, it's time to think again.

Research has shown that hiking can have an amazing impact on your brain; boosting memory, creativity and even helping your mental health that encourages embodiment. Yes, it's become a science. Otherwise known as Earthing

Hence, to inspire you to hit walking more regularly, here are 10 incredible facts about hiking outdoors and its effect on your body mind. Super juicy. Try barefoot if inclined.

* Hiking helps you to learn new skills for navigating your way around new space, and even the simple act of exploring, helps your brain to flourish again, boosts brain plasticity and flexibility and helps functional circuits to form in the brain.

* A sustained amount of time around woodland has also been found to improve the body's immune system and increase energy levels. Which certainly helps to explain the huge popularity of shinrin yoku ('forest bathing') over in Japan, where the healing powers of the outdoors has long been recognised.

* There's some evidence to say that exploring new environments helps those new nerve cells that have just been born from the exercise, be consolidated into the functional circuit within your brain so they can start being used. So, instead of doing the same old walk next time you decide to get outdoors, take on a new route and reap extra rewards.

* Looking for your next big idea? If you really want to help your brain's ability to think differently and be creative, then yep, you guessed it, go for a hike: "Any kind of exercise seems to induce neurogenesis, which is the birth of new brain cells in the hippocampus, which is the key area of the brain involved in learning and memory. Hiking enhances neurogenesis in your brain which allows it to flourish with new nerve cells that help you to see the world in new ways and to think in new ways.

* Anything that allows you to take a break and go to a different space, also allows your brain to think in a different way. As humans, we're primed and

motivated to want to explore and move around to different spaces and environments and find out new things from those environments. So, we follow our natural instincts that we've evolved for, and the deep brain circuitry embedded within our brain, which prompts us to want to do that, then rewards us once we have.

* Something as simple as hiking for half a day could help you get mentally fit when fighting against any mental health issues you may be encountering. In addition, a 2015 study by Stanford University found that spending time in natural environments helped to calm the part of the brain linked to mental illness.

* Regular hiking can also have a major impact on your memory, meaning at the very least you'll be less likely to forget that crucial birthday or anniversary for another year in a row. This is known because some bods at the University of British Columbia made a load of people walk briskly for an hour, twice a week, and found many examples of the subjects' hippocampus growing bigger as a result. Not only does that help with creativity, but that also boosts our ability to remember and learn.

* Believe it or not, going off on a hike to a scenic, natural spot can induce alpha waves to work their magic in your brain with spectacular results. Exercising in beautiful surroundings would induce alpha waves, the slow frequency of brain waves that flow electrically across your brain. They're good for

helping you to think in a calm and maybe creative way as well. There is some indication that if you have higher alpha waves it helps to combat depression.

* In fact, hiking can also cause the brain to release endorphins which can have the effect of decreasing our sensitivity to stress and pain, and also make us feel euphoric. We've all heard runners bang on about those feel-good endorphins they get after smashing a 15km Sunday morning jog – or something along those lines anyway.

* Research has shown that regular walking for a year can have a long-lasting impact on the overall plasticity of the brain, especially in the ageing brain, meaning that potential age-related brain problems can be kept at bay.

How many of them are you aware of? Come on, be honest?

Now imagine going for a naked hike? Can you imagine the total freedom in that, or does the thought fill you with dread? For me, this experience is the cherry on the cake. Total liberation. Why wait for summer solstice and Naked Hiking Day!

Respectfully, nature has a magical way of absorbing overwhelm. It's uber vital to unplug from the matrix often, as our fast-paced way of living is excessively toxic and promotes living in the head. Planting our feet on the ground helps us to connect with our heart, our breath, and acknowledge what is, because it's tough out there sometimes. Bonus, nothing beats the grandness of nature to quieten any feeling of unease. Just being in the mountains makes me realise how small and insignificant I am. I feel held and supported, wild and free. It's almost as if time stands still. Factoring in the water element, especially waterfalls, and river scrambling, is triple healing medicine and mega fun too. Bare foot hiking has become my favourite pastime, squelching in the mud until my toenails are blackened and blue. I know there is a lot of science about it, but to me, I don't need to know all this, I just know that being outdoors in nature is good for me. If I don't go out each day for at least a few hours, I feel incredibly sick. Is this you too?

'It only takes 1 candle to light the fire of a thousand flames.'

Does breathing, breath work and breath holding alone make you feel embodied?

Now that is a great question. For me, I will use the example of surrendering while dipping in extreme icy waters, below 5 degrees, to maximise my longevity. In this instance, of course, an intimate connection to the breath is paramount. Exhaling long, slow and connected to my body, allows me to become present with my body, that any chatter of the mind becomes irrelevant and serene. To the isness of what is. To overcome that cold water rush to the head and over stimulate all those juicy neurons in the head, I immerse myself into an icy river tentatively. To align each and every one of my energy chakra centres as this is a direct connection with the God self. I believe this to be true. One size does not fit all. It's a 1:1 unique communion with nature. Mine looks like a slow immersion, working my way from my root chakra up to my knees, thighs, waist, torso, chest and lastly my exquisite neck, the resting place of my holy vagus nerve. There is indeed, so much science out there, on the benefits of cold-water therapy, but for me it is purely magic. My mind does not need to understand it, I simply need to feel it, connect with it, thank it, and know that on many levels, whatever I am experiencing holds many transferable life skills which needs no mind to apply thought. For instance, if I can muster the courage to immerse myself in an icy, hail stoning lake, I sure as hell can walk into an interview, speak my truth, nail it or not and know that I am within the limitless limitations of life. Whatever the outcome, I will remain happy, balanced and knowing.

What's more, breath work and its counter parts, were my devote principles at the beginning of my journey. More so, in relation to my studies in traditional hatha yoga. A structured approach is the best method to rote learn, until those nursey bike stabilisers require cracking off. Then, in my opinion, an unstructured feminine flow approach, to develop, maintain, and sustain the body minds fine tuning is key to becoming one's own guru. Nothing more.

Some like to dive in at the deep end. Some like it wearing nothing but a birthday suit, some can stay in for ages, some are deeply sensitive and filed with trauma and somehow are so highly sensitive to life and probably feel like a misfit. Water is such an uncanny metaphor for life's sensual pleasures. Although it is important to get the breathing rhythm right, otherwise you may be struck down with cold water shock.

Are you enjoying the ramblings of a crazy lady so far?

What I am trying to say is that embodiment is in the intentional practice, and that comes with a sense of developed awareness. The breath connection is always there and arises consciously or unconsciously, but is activated more fully with intention, such as if you are a weightlifter, runner, swimmer, wind instrument player, deep sea diver, or a yogi performing breath work. Intentional combined moving and breathing practices like the aforementioned, are all spiritual and skilfully connect the mind to the body through the breath. Nor, in my opinion, is it something to attain, but is heightened by our naturalness, if we are in a state of allowing.

I overheard an 82-year-old lady chat about a Saxophone players incredible elongated breathing during puffing through a tricky piece, 'he's no problem with his breathing has he.' Said dear who writhes with COPD. Are you with me?

I'm not on the autistic spectrum. Well maybe? Aren't we all? How many times do you check that you have locked the back door before you go to bed in the evening?

Autism is just part of my Neurodiversity, as is ADHDifference, Dyslexia, hypersensitivity, rejection sensitivity dysphoria and so much more. Unless the government are allowing topping up the mercury and aluminium childhood vaccinations with lethal doses to overtime, change child development. Didn't the CDC recently alter the benchmarks for crawling, walking, and speaking in babies from 12 to 18 months? Thoughts?

Anyways, all these labels and acronyms are fine if it means you can get help, understanding and support. But they stand on their own, they are just words made up by Psychologists and doctors trying to explain why we are different. They separate our behaviours like we are lab experiments and then try and tell us who we are, and what we cannot achieve and how to be more like them. Are we lab rats?

Well, think about this for a moment; It's because we are SUPPOSED TO BE LIKE THIS. Nothing went wrong, nothing bad happened that caused it, no one is responsible for Neurodiversity (or are they?). It is a different brain type that has evolved alongside Neurotypicalness. No one says being Neurotypical is a disorder or condition, or something caused it. It's just accepted as the "norm."

So instead of thinking of autism or ADHD or dyslexia or any of my Neurodiversities as separate "things" I "have." See them like I do, as ONE brain that works incredibly well and to such a high standard that it becomes delicate and can be hurt very easily.

We are not broken, we are not, we are born to be who we are, and only the world and people's attitude towards us should change, not us. Enough thought-provoking spiel. Sorry to go off on a teacher tangent. Let's get back on track with this theme of embodiment in this next to last chapter. I can't help but feel so passionate in the roots of this significant labelled spectrum, wearing my teacher hat.

For me, embodiment is simply using the body as a tool for healing through self-awareness, mindfulness, self-regulation, connection, finding balance and self-acceptance. True embodiment explores the relationship between our physical being and our energy which can be expressed positively and negatively. More importantly, for the feminine, our bodies influence our sense of self, our image and identity. Our culture tends to define a woman by her body.

Botox, bum lifts, tit enhancements, lip augmentation anyone?

Can you sing with affectionate emotion, 'every little cell in my body is happy?'

Daily, as an embodied woman, I religiously refer to my body as a source of guidance. When my yoni is wet and juicy, she is telling me yes. Dry. A firm no. I call her my 4th brain. Even peri menopausal, I kid you not.

For me, embodiment is not prescribed as another something that is 'out there,' to attain. We are all unique flowers in this garden called life and no one size fits all. We are all embodied in a body in our own unique way. Nor should we be made to fit our nature as a square peg into a round hole for the sake of fitting in. Likewise, it is about accepting what is and navigating that in our own, selfish, best interests. Being able to be selfish is a skill set. Rare to most. Its fucking beautiful and sexy when another reflects that back to you.

When I tentatively got into yoga in 2009 after my brother committed suicide, I clearly remember the time when I first started experiencing bizarre energetical random movements. At first, my leg would spasm and uncontrollably jerk, and then my hips started to voluntarily vibrate. After that, I experienced a strange spell of debilitating severe headaches and vision loss. Initially, I rather enjoyed it, until these very strange, mystical, physical manifestations started to increase and affect my day-to-day living.

For instance, drawing upon the time I had to lie in bed for 3 days as my severe cluster headache wore off. I could barely see, everything was soft focus but what I did notice was that the sky had stopped still, the birds were frozen in the sky and the green grass in the garden below was radiating electric currents just like the green and azure blue tones pulsating up and down through my body. I started seeing auras around people too. Mostly reds or purples hazes that blanked out a face. It felt as though I was having a huge body orgasm and I was pumping in sweat. My daughter came into the room once, and I daren't say anything. I just lay there in suspicion. A few days later, at A&E, the Doctors decide that a lumber puncture would be the best option to get a clear indication of my now improving symptoms, albeit worrying. I drop into flight mode after hearing about the procedure. I bailed out. I've always been petrified of any hospital procedures. No idea why.

Another time I was literally thrown out of my bed across the room, dazed and confused while in a deep sleep state. Akin to the time, and for no apparent reason, on a train trip to the seaside, I was thrown around the carriage. Other passengers stared on in disbelief, thinking to themselves 'what a possessed woman.' My cheek was hard pressed to the window with force until I was thrown to the floor and whatever 'it' was, left. Only then was I able to regain my composure and smooth my ruffled feathers and sit myself quietly down on my seat. It looked like a scene out of the Poltergeist.

My most horrendous moment was when I had to take a week off work to stay indoors as I could not stop gushing over the slightest things that made me feel connected to the energy of love. I remember washing my hands with dish soap and feeling this intense love feeling that I spontaneously released. Another time, I went for a jog around the park on a beautiful warm afternoon. Halfway round I was feeling intensely sensitive and connected to all the beautiful, coloured flowers, shrubs and sights and sounds that I, yes, I did, I looked like I'd wet my jogging pants and the by passers didn't half give me evil stares!! I felt mortified. Low and behold, I learnt how to not attach to the experience but just observe it and let it go. It did, after almost 7 days hiding.

Furthermore, I came to the realisation that squirting from my yoni was no different than squirting from my eyeballs. It is just another outlet of expression. The same as the anus is a second mouth. Work that one out.

I also learnt that I am not my body. I know that. I have discovered how to embody, hold, contain, listen intuitively, love, enjoy, act in accordance with what it wants to nourish itself in a moment-by-moment requirement. Nothing more than that. This is what true embodiment looks like to me. I wonder what yours looks like. I'd love to know. It is not a shape, form, class, linear structure or set of logic.

Massage supports the wellbeing of my nervous system functioning too. The importance of touch on my body, of sensual touch to release, relax, restore, and stabilise my precious nervous system in all its labelled departments. Interestingly, are the varied outer body experiences I've encountered with those. One somatic massage put me in a sobbing state for the whole weekend afterwards. Huge energetical release. Of what, the mind does not need to know.

Another time while on the massage table, my angel wings popped out and I was levitating off the bed when my experienced massage facilitator had to come back into her earth body and bring me back from another realm. With conscious awareness. I had a sense that I wanted to go home. I was present both in my body and out at the same time, if that makes sense. Another time, I felt my neck twist halfway round. I felt as though I was a witch and hung in a former life and had to do a specific mediation to address that. To heal that rope sensation felt. Thank you to the Silver Spoon Sisters Collective. You enhanced my awareness of the treacherous goings on in Lancaster, one fine autumnal afternoon. Quite recently, even the MP for Scotland, Nicola Sturgeon has addressed an apology for the horrific slaughter of the Scottish witches in historical times. Bravo.

Coming into the body to support and deeply appreciate the relationship with the bodies needs is what I define as embodiment. Some of these bizarre experiences you may not have had or ever will.

To one therapist, stuck energy within the body may look like trauma, to another shakti kundalini, to another a psychosis manifestation. A deliverance minister may suggest demonic possession. Labels, labels, labels for the mind to make sense of to hang an experience on. Is there such thing as a spiritual crisis? What might be the causes and its manifestations? A spiritual crisis could be understood positively as in spiritual emergence and personal transformation, or as a living nightmare of paranormal phenomenon. Whatever the world view or belief system held, we can experience drastic challenges and changes to our personal meaning system and sense of purpose, identity, and relationships. For example, projections of dead people linked with unresolved bereavement trauma, or poltergeist activity generated unconsciously in response to suppressed mental and spiritual distress.

However, ignoring the body mind spirit needs is like typing with hammers.

The truth will set you free but not until it has finished with you.

-David Foster Wallace

Are you like me and feel your emotional body, more intimately than the brain? Do you serve her well?

With every single ounce of love that she deserves. On every liberating level?

One thing for certain is that being embodied helps us to experience that wholeness of life. By becoming more aware of the subtle sensations means you will gain more sensory clarity and insight. You will start to become more aware of your needs and how to meet them better. Get curious about your body. Get to know it well. The embodied self is our true nature. Our cells, organs and tissues communicate and collaborate with each other and hear every word we tell them in a complex dance.

Think and speak kindly always and in all ways.

Wildest Dreams

Hello friend. Thank you for keeping up with me so far, my lovely companion. It's now 04:15am and yet again, I am woken up by incessant words coming to me in my head that want to be shared and I have listened to the birds tweeting away outside for the last half hour, I'm toasty warm in my bed, while I lovingly share my final words with you.

Not in my wildest dreams did I think that this was possible. Still, I will never be who I once was because of what I have been through. This is our gold; it is hidden in our life's challenges. We each have a story, a book, our very own happy ever after within us, that is called our very own, amazing life. There are always blessings to be found in a crisis.

How to overcome adversity.

I am not who I was 6 years ago. I was a woman who listened to everything others told her she had to do and had never learnt how to listen to my own inner voice. I hid so many parts of myself. I didn't like to be seen and I feared being heard because, what if people didn't like what I had to say? I hid behind the mask of niceness.

I am different now, having gone through my own personal trauma. I have a voice. I don't care what people think of me anymore. I allow myself to be seen — the real me, not the one I think will win people's approval. Yes, I may appear a tad crazy, but this is me and I will not apologise for that.

The truth is challenging circumstances in our lives change us. The death of a child, a toxic relationship, a life-threatening illness, an affair that forced you to face who you really are instead of who you were pretending to be, coming out after an addiction that almost killed you—those things change us.

When these challenges pass through us, emotionally, spiritually, physically, and mentally, we are never, ever the same.

When these things happen in our lives, it forces us to pause, reflect on what we have been through and own who we now are, or who we want to be now that our masks are off.

These experiences happen to us to shake things up, to reveal things that may have been hidden or we just weren't willing to see.

I wanted to be a better version of myself, after my life fell apart when my Dad died. I had to be more compassionate, more understanding, less judgmental and more accepting of myself and my own flaws.

I had to take my pain and learn how to sit with it, and accept, understand and be compassionate through it, without running away, even though the many dark nights of the soul that almost killed me on so many levels. It is what I can only describe as what a junkie must feel like when experiencing cold turkey. Releasing the trauma and wounding stored in the emotional body feels like that. No words but so shuddering many.

There have been many moments in my own process where I wanted to give up.

During my stint in Dubai, I wanted to quietly slip away from the physical body. Yet, something deep within me kept me going. Was it grace? I do not know. Looking back, it was my Dad's Omega watch and the hope of a new way of living which brought me to the realisation that I am worth it. Thanks to my Dad. He was there with me in spirit. I didn't jump. I took the courage to jump within instead.

What I do know is this. Suicide is not about really wanting to be dead. It is about killing what we do not like about ourselves on the inside that really counts.

I am not the same person anymore.

Once you overcome adversity and come to understand the wisdom within your crisis, you will flip that into freedom. You are forever changed from that experience, and then you will discover your new self.

We cannot be sorry to the people in our lives who knew us before because we can't go back to being the person before the crisis. The crisis happened for a reason. We walk forwards in life, never backwards.

We sometimes can't go back into a marriage after we've had an affair, because the affair changed us.

We can't go back to a partner that supported us through an addiction, because what kept us with them in the first place was the addiction itself.

Once you've changed, everyone around you follows suit.

Your energy changes; their energy changes.

Overcoming adversity involves plenty of loving kindness, compassion, and quality alone time. Feeling stuck? Discover how to tune in to the intelligence of your own inner voice, instead of swimming around in circles, stuck in the goldfish bowl syndrome and old programmes of the mind that no longer serve you.

For those going through your own challenges. Expect that you are either going to step up to your full potential or spiral out of control. You cannot fall into line and give in to things that you know are no longer right for you because of what you have been through.

Seek professional, experienced, trauma informed guidance; be courageous enough to be seen, supported, and held in your vulnerability, which will help you grow. Expressing and sharing your vulnerability is your greatest ally. It is the highest form of self-love and takes incredible strength. For certain, is it not a weakness, as we have been conditioned to believe. It is our mark of our humanness, our badge of honour, to wear with pride because of our capacity to love and feel so very deeply.

For me, aliveness became the new super food.

What in the world is wrong with me? Have I gone totally mad?

Over one hundred thousand different thoughts constantly babbling away, like the hum of a radio, continually buzzing in the background, signposting the same negative emotions; anger, sadness, guilt, and fear, backed up and stored in my memory file folder that had built up for more than 40 years. Wasn't this normal?

Although, I didn't have a question or an answer.

Until the day came to finally losing my mind, before eventually, lovingly, re-building it again, only in a much healthier and tender manner. While, losing dear friends and much-loved family along the way. Though, I didn't really lose anything, the form just changed.

Moreover, the only way forward was to commit to listening to, and feeling into, the innate intelligence of my heart and gut brain (and yoni brain), to properly integrate these formerly redundant intelligences with the proper attention and focus I/they deserved, for me to positively move forward in my life.

My accumulated pressure of feelings had built up over far too much time, years and years of thoughts, fear, guilt etc., etc. ... POP ... I found myself detailing and documenting my inner struggles as I travelled the globe in search of how to reclaim my body mind and spirit, a Northern birds account on life, marriage, child rearing, empty nest syndrome, education, sex, God, adventure, relating in mid-life, work, death, grief, and mental health concerns such as, feeling electric energy shooting up my spine, and seeing vivid colours all around me, just who the heck was I? What exactly is this meaning of life? It has been suggested that my story is akin to a humorous eclectic mash up of 'Eat, Pray, Love' 'The Butterfly Effect' and 'On the Road,' but far juicer versions. Often closing the curtains at night and looking up to the stars to wonder if there was more to life?

During my fortunate travels, I discovered that the nature of monkey mind is to relieve pain and suffering, I had so many negative thoughts filed away in my memory folder, that I so wanted to be free of my inner conflict, emotional inner turmoil and limiting beliefs. These had been firmly suppressed inside of me, yet I did not know how to express them properly with my peers or family. Let alone with my G.P! Can you imagine!

Before I embarked on my journey, I remember having terrible mood swings, tight and stiff shoulders and neck issues, emotional drinking and eating habits, weight problems, apathy, irritability, teeth grinding, and projected my anger onto everyone else, 'she is this, she is that he said this and that.' You can imagine the rest. Oh, I loved pointing the finger at everyone else but was I aware of the fingers pointing back at me? Had I ever taken full responsibility for my actions or owned them before? Did I know how? Are we even taught in school?

Like me, you might have tried and found useful:

Tapping yourself out of it
Chakra balancing
Meditation
NLP
Visualisations
Hugging Workshops
Earthing
Vision Boards
Psychology
Hanging upside down
Counselling

Praying
Astral projection
Organic vegan/vegetarian foods/Smoothies/Juicing
Sweat-lodges
Fasting
Laughter Yoga
Acupuncture
Running away to India to find a guru
Shaving half your hair off
Getting your nose pierced
Cold showers
Punching pillows
Reading lots of self-help books
Yoga
Reiki
Subliminal music
Tantra
Essential oils
Massage
Breath-work
Health and wellbeing retreats
10-day Silent retreats
Crystals
Saltwater cleansing Kriya
CBT
5 Rhythms dancing
Chinese herbs
Plant medicines such as the great Mother Ayahuasca
Wild Swimming
Divine feminine workshops
Tree hugging
Angel cards

An endless variety of psychotherapy or self-helping techniques, whichever term you prefer?

Everything comes with a story, and I have since learnt not to focus on the drama. Some people love to feed off this and enable others in the process. That's not for me though. It drains and sickens me, the gossip of it, and energy it requires to pulsate and maintain that dark labyrinth of spiralling uncontrolled-ness. The web of dense ambiguity.
    What I have also learnt is deep appreciation, and to remember and include all the lovely people in my life. My dear Mum for bringing me up and feeding me and looking after me, sending me treasured birthday cards and Christmas cards, showing her unconditional love, even when we fell out. I find it extremely satisfying to dig them out of my treasured pandoras box and lovingly touch them in fond memory, with my aging hands. My kids endearing mis-spelt cute Christmas cards too.
    Thanks to my birth Mother for giving me the gift of life. Instead of feeling entitled, I discovered appreciation. Even now, when I go to the Supermarket and they don't have what I want in, I think WOW! Look at what they have got, there is so much kindness in the world. Westerners have so much yet are so conditioned to focus on the negatives. So often appreciation goes unnoticed unless it has a big, fat bow on it. Every single day we are sustained by others. Everywhere we look we are interconnected in this web of kindness, supported, and sustained by

others while receiving the most benefit from our most challenging situations. Let that sink in for a moment.

People are tricky. Yet to find an appreciation and something meaningful, reverts the sense of meaningless. I had received so much benefit from others that I had simply forgotten, I have been touched by so many lovely people on my journey that I have now befriended those self-sabotaging parts of me, the one who enjoyed playing out the victim or rebel, or the attention seeking little girl who liked to throw her toys out of the pram if she didn't get her own way. A wanted/needed people pleaser wannabe. Not.

It does take great courage to become a kindness seeker, or an agent of happiness.

Aliveness is not found in the places most people look for it, yet is the most powerful superfood.

How do you relax into this? Start to realise the glory in the aliveness of each new day?

My suggestion is to start off in small baby steps. Start off by doing small things every day, which if repeated enough will become a habit, which will become automatic and improve the quality of your life.

Self-loving action is the work

How do you catch a monkey?

Very slowly.

To cultivate a self-loving action is certainly a challenge on every level, seemingly more so whilst, 'awake.'

So, tell me more Mooji Baba, explain to me some more Adyashanti and show me Abraham, how to express myself fully, wide open, from this place, utilising these mystical teachings you share? Any spiritual seeker knows that behind the body, behind the drama, behind the emotion, the feelings, the heart, the anchor; we are all one universal body of I Am presence.

Yet, how does one put this fully into practice and embrace this sentiment and live out a life of true compassion, from the heart, on a day-to-day basis and in every ground hog day moment on this earth?

How does one cope when ones' own elderly, physically and mentally ill Mother, is cracking open a can of beer at 7am in the morning to level herself out? Loaded with anti-psychotics, pain killers and a prescribed concoction of other medical drugs?

True behind the mask, the beautiful, almighty silence of awareness prevails. Not wanting to refer to this as consciousness because minus the 'ness' it's not a noun, therefore, it cannot be made. Otherwise, referred to as simply aliveness, which I prefer.

Why? Think of pasta or clay, both have a common essence, and the duality is real but what we don't know is the essence by which it is all known.

From direct experience through spending time in the Ashrams in the East, a common phrase shared is, 'Tat tvam asi,' essentially meaning, I am that essence, you are that essence, that alone exists...But what is that essence?

It appears that we go around in circles in the West, the term consciousness doesn't seem to appear in history. It is an abstract noun which we try to explore, and refers to the fact that we are aware that we are experiencing and dancing in the matrix of life. I often ponder, what then is a thought made of? Matter? Mind stuff? Chitta? An activity of awareness? Are even then, sensations an appearance of the mind?

'All in the mind,' was a common figure of speech in the 1960's, and I should know because my lovely Mother Doris would repeat this mantra when I pleaded a sickness bug as a child to skip school. I loved to stay at home with her and have her attention all to myself. My brothers and sisters would be in school, and we'd chill together watching The Sullivan's on TV whilst munching on cheese and onions pasties with heaping's on brown sauce on! Delightful, saucy memories.

However, try telling that to a mental health patient. To them, disturbing mind stuff phenomena is real. I feel that a psychiatrist keeps people asleep, treats them for waking up and drugs them asleep again …. Helps to drive them crazy … From direct experience, this drives me crazy too.

What's that hissing noise? I can hear my lovely Mother Doris downstairs, cracking open her second can of beer. The time? It is now 7:45am. God bless her. Nondual duality? This is her path and my blessing. So, I will go downstairs and put the previous nights' empty cans in the recycling bin. I will offer her a cup of tea, and a boiled egg, she loves those, and make sure she is comfortable. She might even like a shower, as she was tickled pink the other day when I helped her in to wash her feet, she giggled as she told me that, "She felt like Jesus," as I was soaping her feet.

If we're lucky too, we might grab a bit of fresh air and go around the block for some much-needed scooter training. She still hasn't mastered the right from the left or the snail or hare settings yet! This one time in boot camp I took her into town on it, with my nephews, and she crashed into a full display of shoe boxes, clipping my youngest nephews' leg as they all came tumbling down on top of us! She found this hysterical! You should have seen the shop lady's face! She is such a mischievous bunny!

Later, I will, yet again, speak with her professional team and my sisters. I will not judge, I will accept, and I will practice self-loving action, moment by moment. Why?

Because I Love ... BEing the BEST version of ourselves in the moment.

Thank you, my lovely Mother Doris. Did I tell you enough that I LOVED YOU? No, I didn't.

I MISS you every day my darling Mum. I am not referring to my biological Mum as I do not have reverence for her, but compassion and understanding. I cannot imagine what she went through or has had to live with for all these years. That's letting go happening in an ultimate form. Releasing your own baby when you felt no other choice.

'Blood is not thicker than water.' Doris again.

You may find yourself reaching for a movement practice to cultivate Mindbody wellbeing like Thi Chi, Judisu, Karate, Fencing, cycling swimming or the like. Anything performed with intention has a significant impact on the soul. Intention versus imagination, you choose which word brings you the clearest clarity.

For me, my medicine began with Yoga. The original source on my pathway to self-love and healing.

Hatha also means "to strike a pose," like the Madonna song.

Meaning to strike the body with the challenge of the postures and to "yoke" (the meaning of yoga) the mind into singular focus.

Most styles of yoga in the West are based in Hatha with different philosophies, practices, and terminology that allow yoga to fit the individual practitioner.

Just how many branches are there today? Goat, Beer, Gin, Broga, Doga, Naked, or Silent Yoga Disco? Oh wait, that's my cheeky tipple!

Whatever the branch, ultimately the root of yoga are the principles of how we live our life. Not in stress or overwhelm by today's climate.

My favourite bit, not dogmatised or steeped in religion, are The Eight Limbs of Yoga. These form a moral or ethical code to help us live happier, more meaningful lives. The yoga of balance which, if you are into star signs, as a Libran, thus my favourite form!!

Yama is the first of the 8 limbs and to me, the most important one, which means "restraint." The five Yamas are ahimsa (non-violence), satya (truthfulness), asteya (not stealing), brahmacharya (moderation) and aparigraha (not hoarding). Though, the 10 beneficial commandment laws that were given by the Creator God to show us how to live a better life, work much better for my belief system.

Incidentally, there are amazing yoga schools out there that are non-corrupt or exercise cohesive control. Ask Patanjali. There is always and, in all ways, an opposite force. The trick is to discern which wolf you are feeding. Be mindful of the traps and trust your bodies innate intelligence. Although living in the head is predominant these days and most people do know how to trust the bodies whispers of wisdom. Our fast-paced, current climate promotes wanting more and BEING less.

Yoga's benefits affect each person in a different way. Many find that it helps them to relax; others find themselves feeling healthier and more energetic. All the systems in the body -from the lymphatic to the digestive to the cardiovascular - benefit from yoga. Yoga benefits every aspect of our bodies, inside and out.

On the inside, yoga enables relaxation. Many practitioners find that yoga helps them to focus and feel relaxed in both work and play.

In 2003, scientists studied both long-time yogis and beginners; they found that the stress hormone cortisol had decreased, even after just one session of yoga. Yoga has also been found to increase alpha and theta waves in the brain, meaning that yoga can relax the brain and increase access to the subconscious and emotions. And by simply increasing the feel-good brain chemicals like endorphins, enkephalins, and serotonin, yoga practitioners just feel better.

On the outside, yogis look terrific. This is probably from improvements on the inside! Since yoga balances the metabolism and provides exercise, many find yoga brings their body into balance. Physical yoga strengthens and tones the muscles while improving balance and posture. And yoga is a great way to cross-train for other sports; it can ease strains from injuries and increase strength and flexibility.

Yoga truly is a good egg, and without a doubt, a firm foundation for body mind health. A perfect accompaniment to my love of wild swimming, hiking, and running, that this, half a century years young, body just loves in contrast, while in harmony with the seasons, promoting health and wellness, and celebrating living a full life, rich in aliveness.

No eggy on this face. How do you love yours?

Once I surrendered into the practice of true yoga, I found myself with an open space in my mind to allow more words to flow through me, like these:

I am a Godly crone,
I am no match for your ego mind,
I am a wild woman with a fierce heart,
I am a free, tree spirit,
Father Sky,
Mother Earth,
Harm my children and I promise you,
I will tear you down,
I will scratch your eyes out,

I will not stop,
Until I mirror that darkness within your soul,
Then scratch your eyes out.
Take note,
My life experiences to date,
I am no shrinking violet,
Watch out,
I am a Godly crone.
How can mindfulness inspire you eh?

Life is right now.
    What have you cultivated space for?
    Mary, Mary, quite contrary, how does your garden grow?
    What next? Well after my body mind started opening, due to the trauma being released bit by bit from it, and I started softening into the feminine flow, plus as those hardened shackles started slipping away, I am excited to announce that I literally fell into Wild swimming.
    Wild swimming certainly is a fantastic way to have a mini- adventure close to home, with little kit and clutter. Inspired by my passion for nature, water and minimalism, and the desire, to do something challenging and new. Hence, I came up with the idea of trying wild swimming, accidentally on purpose.
    When you slip into the waters of a shimmering ocean, swim along a willow-lined river or plunge into a mountain waterfall, you are doing more than just enjoying one of nature's greatest and healthiest highs. You are opening a whole new world of magical adventures – adventures that are abundant

in in our wet and sea bound country and bring on a whole new way of exploring our landscape.

I love the idea of secret swimming spots just waiting to be discovered. Often, finding out the best swimming spots are not on 'Google' but in what the Germans call wanderlust. The best spots are to be found in an organic way, through a pub conversation, a fellow rambler, or a fellow wild swimmer, it's like discovering some kind of unofficial folk wisdom because it isn't written down.

For me, the right to swim in the UK's waterways should be as equal to the right to roam the lands.

My own wild swimming adventures began in a Huckleberry Duff kind of way, growing up on the canals and riverbanks in Lancashire, learning to swim in the canals, building rafts and rope swings and camping out on the riverbanks. So, quite naturally, I feel as though I'm going back to my childhood and feeling like an eight-year-old kid again.

Over the last few years, I have been seeking the perfect wild swimming place.
I think, waterfalls are my favourite natural place to start, a place where nature is at its most powerful, sculpting and carving incredible jacuzzi pools for jumping and diving. In a way it all started here, in Yorkshire, in Ingleton Falls and Janet's Foss, where my ex-husband and I would visit with our tiny tots. I love waterfalls also because they have mystical qualities. To our pagan and Christian forefathers to be immersed in water, to enter a pool, was to cross a threshold, and enter the spirit world.

In my wild swimming journey, I aim to seek the highest and wildest mountain wild swimming places too. To date, my favourite is Wastwater, also Britain's deepest lake, under its highest mountain. The beaches are made of white quartz, and it has the clearest water in the whole Lake District. Although, on my 'Tad Dah' list is to trek up the mountain to Lamb Dub, Britain's highest tarn. However, I must say, Britain highest beach at Gadding's Dam is rather exhilarating and extremely impressive. (Look out for me in the Wild Water Swim film, out soon!)

Perhaps stepping away from the challenges of modern-day living, and doing something that brings us closer to nature sounds appealing? Do you love the idea of stripping off all your clothes and immersing yourself into a cold body of water, to commune with it and understand your why? In doing so, it can bring you closer to nature and the world beyond the day to day.

Wild swimming does have its potential hazards just like anything else, but with full awareness of them, like knowing how to spot the dangers, swimming sober, swimming with others, gradual exposure, breathing techniques, no jumping (gasp reflex) and recognising signs of drowning and being prepared for it, then there really are only the benefits to enjoy.

There really is something spiritual about plunging into cold water and surfacing to be confronted by beautiful surroundings, in a way, maybe we are born again?

Shh, listen silently to your earth body,
Can you hear?
The wisdom it holds to whisper.
Do you enjoy your naked body?
For the sake of pure enjoyment,
Relishing in its exquisite beauty.
Letting go of sexual objectivity,
Letting go of judgement,
Whole as you are,
Magic in aliveness,
Held within the intuitive wisdom of him,
of her, of them or their,
It has been silenced for way too long,
Wild hearted soul.

I am not who I was 6 years ago.

I will never be who I once was, because of what I have been through. This is our gold; it is hidden in our life's challenges. We each have a story, a book, our very own fairy-tale, happy-ever-after within us, that is our very own, amazing life.

Sex and Suicide.

A tad random, I agree, but that is me and it is not what I had faithfully planned.

On a beautiful, sunny afternoon, while driving home from a Papyrus Suicide Fundraiser, I experienced a profound realisation. Thank you for allowing me to share them with you. They unfolded like this:

During a conversation, with other kind-hearted empathies, I realised just how open I was and non-fearful about sharing my insights around this devastating topic or the destruction that it brings. On how, drawing from my own experience, support and openness is vital to those left behind, so they DO NOT feel stigmatised, guilty, or shameful. I came to see my own strength and knowledge.

Dealing with grief is enough to contend with, as losing a dear one in these tragic circumstances certainly causes a traumatic response through the whole-body mind, which can last for years. Some never get over this form of loss. One never expects a child to pass before an adult/parent either.

Nonetheless, nothing and no thing is permanent in this life. Life is always unfolding, changing, moving, growing, shedding, revealing, and forming the new, mirroring nature as that is what we are until our own time for our bodies to leave this planet arrives. I have no idea if there is another place that we go to, or if reincarnation is real, but I do know that I haven't met anyone else who has come back to tell me, have you? It makes me laugh when I read on Twitter, how well-known Gurus bang on about reincarnation and everlasting life. How do they know where any one of us go upon death? If anywhere at all? Have they tried and tested it out?

Although, I feel my Mums energy a lot, mostly when out walking or running, as the breeze caresses my face, that feels reassuring and makes me feel alive, held, and loved. I will often open my arms out to the sun and say an inner thank you too. This may sound a bit odd, but she also loved Red Robins and said that she'd come back as one if she could. Guess what? I spot them often when outdoors, flitting in and out of the shrubbery, and I'll always stop for a little natter just in case it is her spirit animal.

To add, earlier today at this wonderful event, I had a lovely conversation with a male, Baptist Church Youth Worker, who commits himself each week to helping disadvantaged boys. He spoke about structure, safe zones, boundaries, and clear communication, which is at the forefront of the work the charity does. I felt humbled, to be with such a kind group of humans, who are, without a doubt, real life saints by today's standards. Not looking for praise, not uploading a pic for social media, but doing and being the 'real work.'

In a world full of fake, realness is rare.

On the contrary, I also discovered that at my age, (late starter to the party) just how far I had come on my own journey, of stripping back and peeling the onion layers since the start of 2015. Incidentally, there's so much of my past self that I don't recognise anymore, but I love her just the same. She was growing, she was doing her best, and she fought hard times to get me here.

Not what I had exactly planned!!

I do not like to use the term 'healing' to describe my journey, I do not know what that means but what I do know is that if cut my finger with a sharp knife and it bleeds, then it will need time to repair or heal itself. Using the term to heal, especially in-front of children I feel is harming, conditioning them to perceive you to be sick, not good, unworthy, lacking in something. I prefer to use the terms; allowing, surrendering, or feeling into what is coming up in the body mind, which I feel has a more positive impact in a lifelong manner.

I've since learnt, how to listen to the wisdom of my bodies intelligence and when I sit quietly enough, I can clearly grasp the difference between the mental chatter and the stillness within and a truer reality. Underneath all the conditioning is the true self. If that makes sense?

It makes me giggle when so many use gadgets to meditate, when for me, there is only a quiet space, your body, breath, and awareness needed to join the bash. People will use all kinds of things to increase their ability to accomplish things, but why use them? Why would you wear glasses, use a walking stick or a wheelchair if you didn't need to? With meditation, other than a coming to know what it is and what it can do for you, nothing more than a desire to do so is needed. Painting legs on a snake does not make it walk any better.

However, because we live in an ego society, we are taught to chase status, labels, things, all the things outside of us. Wearing a mask, hiding our true nature, seeking approval of those who conditioned us to think we need it. Life is not a competition.
I've eaten organic oats with almond and turmeric milk for brunch today. That's rock and roll enough for me.

Now for the sex bit:

I'm a woman, mother, and grandmother, in addition to a 6-year unravelling of self to my name, that included travelling the globe in search of reclaiming my body, mind, and spirit. I can only share from my experience, as that is what I know to be true. Not the absolute.

'After a deeper understanding of life, I found out what's possible when you are safe to let down your guard completely and love yourself in totality. '

After experiencing my own profound awakening session in the skilled hands of a Russian practitioner on a holy Thai island, revisited in my first book, mentioned in my Twin Flames chapter, and delving some more into my own cervix self-enquiry.
 Here are some of my findings:
 Did you know that the cervix is a gateway for profound pleasure states?
 The cervix is usually medicalised, poked, and prodded or associated with birth.
 In fact, the cervix is a beautiful part of the female sexual anatomy.
 But no one talks about it like this.
 The cervix is highly innervated. It is supposed to feel pleasure! And yet for many women it is numb or painful to touch. Why? Mainly due to premature penetration, invasive medical procedures or disassociation caused by shame or abuse.
 In the global online project, Self: Cervix, they discovered that not only is it possible to recover

sensation and heal the cervix but it's also possible to trigger the most transcendent orgasms possible.

WHY THE CERVIX?

The cervix is attached to the 10th cranial nerve, the Vagus nerve. The vagus goes directly to the pineal gland, bypassing the spine. Within the orgasmic state participants can experience the release of DMT - the active ingredient found in plant medicine such as Ayahuasca. Cue, cosmic bliss attained through lovemaking transitory blacking out.

Cervical orgasms can be profound and life changing.

Also, cervical stimulation without orgasm can positively affect a woman's energy levels, creativity and sense of confidence.

WHY DOES THIS MATTER?

When a woman begins to pay attention to her cervix, the way she makes love to herself, and others begins to change. The process creates new sensitivity and awareness in the area. This new connection forges new pleasure pathways or strengthens what she already knows. Her concept of orgasm begins to change and expand. She begins to take charge of how she's entered and by whom, because she learns the impact of crossing her own boundaries; it shows up in her cervix and vagina as tension, pain, or numbness.

The more aware you become of your sexual energy, and the more you start to meditate on this, the more you will start understanding, that the sexual energy itself is profound, and it is exquisitely beautiful. The more you start nurturing this flame from deep inside your own soul, the more you start to understand just how profoundly beautiful it is, in many of its manifest forms, it doesn't necessarily mean plugging in either, sexual energy can be used in other creative outlets, it is not purely the act itself.

True awakening of sexual energy comes with the true understanding of the energy forms and the way it manifests in our lives.

Modern society worships youth and its bodily form, without understanding that without maturity at SOUL level, the physical form is but a vessel and an empty one at that.

The younger generation of today are far more open and aware due to the wide-open door of the World Wide Web, isn't it about time that our National Curriculum moved into the 21st Century and instead of a highly focused cognitive curriculum; emotional intelligence, including self-enquiry and self-regulation was incorporated to provide a more balanced, wholehearted, wholesome, enriched, loving curriculum in line with our modern-day living? You'd probably get kids far more engaged and curious, even wanting to go to school in the morning, eager to learn, instead of scraping them off their beds! Also, are we equipping our future generation with the right tools to live well in their own skin? As energy, maybe still monetary, (who knows?) will exchange in ways we have no idea of yet. Are we breeding a nation of overweight, stay-at-home, transfixed, sugar addicted, gamers?

I can't bang on about this enough, as the brilliant philosopher Aldous Huxley, over a century ago, stated this requirement! So, before we dehumanise ourselves altogether, let's reconnect with our reality by including fundamental topics, previously hidden in the closet with the skeletons, such as sex and suicide.

Well, maybe not in the same context, my intention is not to sound severe, but you get my drift on raising standards. The current sex education in the UK is still as maladroit as ever, I've first-hand knowledge from my nephews! Nor is the subject of death properly embedded. Is this what Ofsted define as 'enriched curriculum provision?' Is this why there is so much stress in education today and long-term staff absences? It's so outdated and draconian. No wonder kids are high as kites in the classroom, and teachers don't know what to do with them. The old ways have hit the highways.

Plus, with studies revealing an increase in narcissism personality traits due to over exposure on social media, it is becoming difficult for many to navigate this thing called life. Who can you trust, or speak to, who can you be yourself around and be goofy with, without judgement? Without fear of something circulating the WWW? Likewise, who is your God? Your idol? With so many New Age, spirituality, self-made gurus and various messages leaking out there, what is ethical or morally right or wrong anymore, do you know your highest values, are they even yours? Are you genderless, is that ok to ask even? Do you think our kids still believe that God sits on a white cloud in the sky with a matching white beard? Who am I and who are you?

In a nutshell:

Are we setting up a future generation with the right tools to be mentally, spiritually, emotionally and physically wealthy?

I remember, while teaching primary children about loss, and the darkness that it brings, that it brought about many thoughts of fear.

I've learnt that owning our stories of heartbreak is a huge challenge in a culture that 'tells' us to deny our heartache, our vulnerability, and probably not something that you would bring up in conversation at the dinner table with your Grandparents, Aunty Marge or Uncle Billy is it, or is it?

I love Brené Brown's message on becoming vulnerable and having the courage to put yourself out there.

So, today has been an insightful one to say the least. I've certainly come (no pun intended) a long way inwards these last 6 years. I'm feeling rather thankful for that, so I'm going to celebrate with a chai tea and lavender bath with beeswax candlelight.

I hope your universe is glowing.
What is time?
The time is now.
Slowing down,
Cultivating quiet,
Starting the day with intention,
Ending the day with prayer,
It is time to get deeply serious above love and self-loving action.
It is easier to cultivate around others doing the same,

Coming together with others in a holy space,
Joined in love and devotion,
A field of love magnified that lifts all members into a higher vibration,
Modern lifestyles falling prey to the noise of distraction,
Modern lifestyles falling prey to Monkey Mind thoughts,
Silence is the muscle we must build up,
It is time to get deeply serious about love and self-loving action,
To transform energies,
To hear our inner voice,
To build love on love,
Not fear on fear,
Beware, the cheeky Monkey Mind will put up an enormous battle to stay,
Bravely surrender,
Return to the core of BEing,
The Monkey Mind will sneak back in and push a knife through the heart of a drama,
Or steals someone's dreams.
It is time to get deeply serious about love and self-loving action,
The time is now,
That time is now,
This time is now.

Unless it isn't.
    Why?
        You've heard of the Comfort Zone, right?

It's a place we feel comfortable, and I've been hammering on about this throughout this unfolding story so far.

We have a Comfort Zone in everything - food, tasks, driving routes, and especially the people we associate with. Oh yes, you know the score!

A few years ago, I went to the gym and chatted with the most popular guy in our school. He was handsome, charming, and yes, captain of the rugby team back in my high school days.

"Nigel how are you?" I asked. "Actually, I'm terrible," he replied. I was really surprised. "What happened to you?"

"I'm going through a traumatic divorce. Not only have I lost the person I love most, but since we cocooned and spent all our time together, I don't have a support system now."

Then Nigel brought up the Comfort Zone. His theory?

"We find one person who knows all our insecurities. That person becomes our Comfort Zone, so we spend most of our time with that person. We don't challenge ourselves to hang with new people or do new things." The Comfort Zone simplifies life.
You don't need to exert effort or thought when you're inside it. The problem is, the Comfort Zone becomes a habit. It seduces us because we start to confuse comfort with happiness. The moment this happens, we stop challenging ourselves. Does this make sense to you?

Of course, the Comfort Zone saps our confidence because we're not evolving ourselves.

We're basically coping with life. How do you know the Comfort Zone is getting you?

There are four signs. One is boredom. Your life feels repetitious and without novelty. Another is restlessness. You wonder, "What's it all means?" A third is underachievement. There's a niggling feeling in the back of your mind that you were meant for more.

A final one is inertia. When you think about moving outside the comfort zone, it feels exhausting. The good news is that it's easy to move outside your Comfort Zone once you realise it's limiting you. Ah, those limiting beliefs again.

However, there are two steps for moving yourself out of the Comfort Zone fast.
The first is obvious. You DECIDE to act.

You decide to do the one thing that will give you the most momentum on your goals today. (Don't worry about tomorrow. Today is all that matters).

Deciding is huge. In the words of Amelia Earhart, the first woman to fly across the Atlantic solo, "The most difficult thing is the decision to act; the rest is merely tenacity. You can do anything you decide to do. You can act to change and control your life, and the process is its own reward."

The second step is activating the burning desire inside of you to be more. To do this, I suggest you tap into your pride. Ask yourself, "What contestant is ahead of me? Who is achieving more than me because he's been willing to do things I haven't been?"

Imagine this person in your mind, and you'll tap into your pride instantly, and with enough motivation to kickstart yourself into action.

The third step is, take control of your confidence, mental toughness, and inner game.

Then you will wake up in the morning with unceasing energy and happiness, excited to tackle the day ahead and take the necessary steps to plan accordingly.

We cannot grow if we do not try new things, for we will always get the same if we always do the same. So, my question for you today is, 'do you practice your values or simply process them or shut them down?'

Do you choose courage over comfort to unleash your curiosity, and explore the ins and outs of your story, because when we walk through our stories to evaluate them, like a three-legged stool, investigating our emotions, thoughts and behaviours, that's were meaning and wisdom live, for it helps us to investigate how we think, feel act about our whole selves?

Otherwise, if we keep everything inside until we can't sleep, eat, work because we are too anxious or depressed, which is our bodies way of reacting to stockpiles of hurt, we are putting ourselves at risk.

Would you walk out on your family, put a backpack on and travel the world in search of how to reclaim your body, mind and spirit as I did and risk losing everything? Your husband, your home, your job, your car, your kids? Your pets? Your money? Your security?

Why?

After my Dad died, I just couldn't cope anymore, I was stockpiling the hurt and couldn't get out of bed, that is until the body spoke, enough is enough.

We have so much wisdom in our bodies if we learn how to listen and trust in what we are hearing. In his book, The Body Keeps the Score, Bessel Van Der Klock, a psychiatry professor, explores how trauma reshapes the brain and body. For us to reclaim our lives and address the relationship between our emotional well-being and our bodies, before the body decides enough is enough, we must shut down the stockpiling and choose courage over comfort.

Having the courage to walk through our stories and rumble them, as Brené Brown lovingly puts it, is a new path to writing our own stories to create new beginnings, a path that leads to whole heartedness.

Owning our story, taking ownership for our emotions is where the revolution starts.

There has never been a more perfect time in our history to stop, look at who you are, decide what you want to change, and start the inner work.

I am nothing like the person I was before my own transformation.

I read, set intentions, meditate, visualise, drum, primal scream, speak truth, practice breathwork, yoga, tantra, wild swim, bare foot hike, dance or BE whatever else it takes to reclaim my body mind, my thinking and feeling, to change my outcomes in life. Not only to love the woman I am becoming, but so that I can love and support another too, from the heart space and in tune with the feminine flow. As an 'embodied' woman. I understand and maintain real friendships too with both sexes. I am wholly seen.

What does that all mean?

It means that I am tune with the natural rhythms of my beating heart. Is she wants to go naked hiking, she will, if she wants to sing wildly in an open lake, she will, if she wants to dance naked around an open fire, she will, if she wants to bang to the beat of the drum at the top of the highest mountain, she indeed will. You see, there is no set pattern, rhythm or rhyme anymore, it is a natural, spontaneous flow of what wants to happen in any given moment. If for example, the negative ions of a free, flowing, icy cold waterfall are desired to boost the mood, that will happen, if the stillness of a lake to self soothe a troubling day is needed, that will happen too. The is so much science and research out there right now about the benefits of cold-water therapy, that deep down, it's really magic.

Our environment is seductive. Latch on to your limitless and be a star of your own story.

Beyond Gratitude for my healing and transformative journey to positivity and self-understanding. Never in my Wildest Dreams would I have thought that I had the ability of writing a second book. If I can do it, so can you. We all have a story within us to tell. I know how difficult life can feel at times. I know what it feels like to be stuck in a challenging chapter, in the past, unable to let go or create the new.

We are not our story, yet they certainly shape us, make us. Or break us.

May my own story, help you with yours. The truth is, the more vulnerable and truthful I became, the more my heart cracked open to let the light in and simultaneously respect the dark.

Lovely quote.

Breathe, Darling. This is just a chapter. It's not your whole story. S.C. Lourie.

Real change takes time and focus, along with a burning desire to let go of old habits that keep you stuck, to recreate a newer version of your future, most natural, at ease, soul self. But change will not happen if you are running on old programmes of the past. The body mind must fire and rewire new networks to do that. This takes time and space. Often, the mid-life transformation, shakes us up with death or disease in which we have no choice but to re-evaluate our inner landscape. Seek out Dr Joe Dispenza on his wisdom. Please be kind on yourself and remember that Rome wasn't built in a day.

And finally, I will love you and leave you with my top tips for health, wealth, and longevity:

* Most of our life is spent chasing false goals and worshipping false paradigms. The day you realise that, is the day you really start to live.

* You really, truly cannot please all the people all the time. Please you first and your loved ones second, everyone else is busy pleasing themselves anyway, trust me. Remember this? JOY? It is an acronym for Jesus first (that is you) Others next and Yourself last (in my world Jesus is also in part YOU!)

* Fighting the ageing process is like trying to find hens teeth. Go with it, enjoy it. Your body is changing, but it always has been. Don't waste time trying to reverse that, instead change your mindset to see the beauty in the new.

* Everyone is perfectly imperfect, and nobody is truly happy with their lot. When that sinks in you are free of comparison and free of judgement. It's truly liberating. Know that to be true.

Easier to say I know, harder to actualise, but possible.
  Loving and leaving you some more with this meaningful, little scribbling:

The ground of understanding
There is always something to be thankful for.
My kids have flown the nest,
My husband is now my Ex,
My parents have gone,
My dog too.
My body is well,
My mind struggles some days,
I feel lots of sadness sometimes,
I use helping techniques and other ways,
To allow this to pass through me,
Like the clouds passing in the sky,

Bravely facing the impermanence.
We cannot experience one emotion without the flip side of another,
How else would we come to know happiness? Sadness?
Or any other emotion fully, for that matter?
That's it.
Nothing and everything matter on this ground of understanding.

Ending my ramblings, the last few years for us all have been penultimately challenging to navigate to say the least. Just like you, I have endured many painful, compulsory transitions. For me, I have broken and tumultuous relationships with the ones I love dearly. The most heart-breaking for me, was not being able to fully support my only daughters first pregnancy and birthing of a new gift into the world. The intensity of not meeting in alignment with one's own inner compass, morals and belief systems while staying non-judgemental between the difference of opinion has been deeply fractious. Our differences make us unique, lest we forget our sameness, our heart coherence connection. How much more pain should we allow to endure? For whom and what?

The mark of the beast?

What entities were throwing parties, celebrating, and enjoying drinks while the rest of us were confined and locked in, and who could not see or visit our dying, or elderly in care? Inhumane. I will not go into another heart-breaking story I know about a severely neglected, mentally ill woman who died because of this absurdity, she was only in her mid-forties, left alone with just her heavily sedating medication for 4 whole months, rotting to death. I know you prefer to be known as Bea, as your real name Joleen re-traumatises you. This kept you in a mental intuition for all your living years because you were not heard properly. Another little self-harming flower, given Electric Shock Therapy, for a crime committed on her by an older man until you were deemed insane. Just know this, and the thousands of others that passed cruelly. I send you love. As do so many other souls roving here on this plane.

Beyond belief.

This book will hopefully help you to venture into the deepest corners of your mind, to stay there and look at your demons, the black wolf, the ego mind, the monkey mind, the shadow part, the wounded inner child part, call it what you will. Only the brave and courageous are willing to go to the depths of themselves and look in the mirror.

How much are you willing to sacrifice, and how much do you want to fly? Can you integrate both your dark and light aspects to maintain and sustain all your brain's coherence? To flex that precious resilience muscle daily, to live and bathe in your own truth, in kindness and compassion to yourself first and others second? Remerging JOY for community?

In sharing my own truth, I hope that it will help you with yours. I hope that you will gather some tools and thoughts and inspirations to navigate your own road map in life. My words support non-violent communication, with no tenacity to hurt anyone. Far from it, written with the highest intention of love, growth, unity, and abundance for all.

Double dare you.

Butterfly woman, womb man, may your own butterfly wings find the courage to blossom, and I mean truly be given permission to bloom and ignite that spark within you, to open your patient butterfly expansive, gorgeous, multi-orgasmic, cosmic wings. They really are waiting to be spread wide open, so that the miracle, which is uniquely unicorn you, designed exclusively for you, can be appreciated. Revealed to the whole of humanity in a peaceful, loving, and harmonic way of living and breathing together, to 'conspire' in conspiracy, winky face. In celestial, juicy union.

Don't forget to let go, this is important, otherwise you will not be fully able to receive your wonderment. Open your heart to recognise the knowledge and wisdom in the lower realms, draw creativity and inspiration from the upper worlds of light and love, alchemically catalyse that into an integration on this path of matter here on this living and breathing mother earth of ours. This is the most important lesson that I've learned, as most spiritual seekers look up to love and light in the first instance but after reading my darkness chapter, may you feel into your own and find the incredible wisdom that lies within that material. For there is a vast amount which must not be shoved under that carpet of shame and blame but held safely and kindly under the candle of compassion. This information will guide you onto your own path to serve others as a much-valued stich in this fabric entitled life. That's what people with a shared vision, living in rich communities do. For example, by having community grocery outlets bridging the gap between food banks and supermarkets, by helping residents with their weekly food shops due to feeling the financial impact of rising living costs.

Small changes, big results over time.

These pioneers are learning to harmonise. Instead of local councils wasting more taxpayer's money on putting more steel fences up around schools and homes and ripping up driveways with concrete and asphalt jungles, let's plant seeds and more trees and recombine as stronger support networks for one another. Like back in the day when you Aunty Marge popped in to borrow a cup of sugar, but the door was never locked, and your Aunty Marge was never your real aunty. Why not uphold one another, take accountability for one another with love and grace. To be encapsulated to the moon and beyond with the butterfly element, or they, them, or she, he, or theirs.

Sounds fanciful I know but a reality if we all were led properly with a genuine heart centred government, without forced into being a tin hat rebellion, and given the opportunity to be given much more beneficial choices to support a healthier longevity on the planet for all, on all levels. Living freely in a society whereby people knew themselves, their sexuality, their creativity, their mind body connection, and energy more intimately, without judgement but in open acceptance, safety, and trust?

With more trauma informed individuals in every profession to forge a more peaceful and loving society.

Wouldn't that be epic?

For me, as a schoolteacher with oodles of years teaching experience in education, nobody ever taught us about how to love ourselves or why that is so important.

Just the other day I was taking a cold dip high in the hills with a dear friend. In the distance we noticed 2 naked young women fondling and gently kissing in the shallows of the water. This was such beautiful living art interaction to observe in the glimmering sunlight, shining down on their luminous skin, blowing hair and glorious mounds. Sadly, I immediately noticed how, as a society we hide love yet celebrate war. You only must turn the tv or radio on and this brain washes you, the destruction element.

Isn't that a sad truth?

Like me, do you love to get lost in time and space when the continuum of time seems to stop effortlessly still?

That for me is peaceful and in alignment with my highest self. Staying away from 'still' people. Still complaining, still hating, still nowhere inside. Attract people into your life who have a bigger vision than you, are more experienced than you, wealthier than you, out of your league completely. You need to be exposed to new levels to go to new levels. This concept that I noticed used to freak me out at first, that is until I devised a little handy visual trick.

Imagine the person next to you sitting on the toilet scrolling on their phone, pants around the ankles. Works every time that sneaky voice comes in saying, 'oi, you're not good enough.'

Drop that old chestnut, that old limiting belief of, I'm not good enugh.

For most people, the one major aspect of their lives that stops them achieving so much more is the BS story they keep telling themselves, every day. And I know this all too well.

This endless, auto-play message of 'I'm simply not good enough,' and 'what will other people think' or perhaps for you it's 'I'm too old, too young, not educated enough, too educated, too busy, too scared, too broke' (Pick one).

Another handy hack to help you navigate when you are out of synch. I'll use my reference point to help you understand more. I know when I am out of alignment with my highest self as I fall straight back into a few old self-sabotaging patterns. When I am in it, I am aware that this 'disgusts me,' yet at the same time I know that it is a learnt response and coping mechanism when faced with a bigger life challenging moment to contend with. I have 2 of them intertwined and I haven't been able fully to get rid of them because, on a positive note, when they come up and are re-enacted, this is my signal for, 'oh no, somethings out of whack.' Then cue, mindful recalibration.

Small daily challenges, I am more able to witness, meet and not merge with. I've fine-tuned that skill. Thank the universe. No adverse reactions or unwanted behaviours.

With this insight and shining loving awareness onto the big boys of triggers, I can quickly sit with it until it passes, like the clouds passing in the sky, nothing is fixed but transitionary and temporary. Nor do I beat myself up about it if I get caught in the trap. I know this is part of our human condition and perfect imperfection. The labyrinth of the mind can be a devilish mercenary you know. Plus, I know that I must get out of my own way to allow what wants to come to me, for what wants to happen arise, without procrastination. Expressing healthy anger has been the most challenging. How is this expressed for you?

Furthermore, without self-awareness and boundaries be careful with whom you share your sensitivities with. Do not become a dumping ground for others at your autonomy.

Whatever your story is, make today the day you change it by owning it. The whole damn lot.

Live your wildest dreams. But first, to do that, it is essential that get out of your own way.

Spread your cosmic wings Butterfly Woman, and dare fly, fly, fly.

And remember too, to remind yourself daily about the wolf that you are choosing to feed. Is one of them receiving more attention? Get clear.
AAAAoeWWW. ROOOOAARRRR.

Lest to forget that what you seek is also seeking you. I've put an order in to God with an appeal for a brand-new golden world arising out of love, unity, and a trauma-informed community.

What's your request?

I love you more than you will ever know sis-STARS.

These are my words.

Sending love and blessings to all, as above, so below.

P.S. Dear loving spirt of the universe, may I be blessed to connect with my daughter and her first special miracle, and my first blessed granddaughter by the time this book goes to print. I promise not to kill any more nuns! Brownie Promise!

P.P.S. We each have our crosses to bare and wishes to fulfil.

P.P.P.S.
God,
Send your peace,
Peace to this world,
Peace to this country,
Peace for my friends and my community,
Peace for my family and loved ones,
God, give me your peace,
And then help me to give it away.
Thank you.
Amen.